Stoneflies and Turtleheads

A Maine Flyfisher's Misadventures

D. Dauphinee

STONEFLIES & TURTLEHEADS

A Maine Flyfisher's Misadventures

ISBN 978-0-945980-50-6

Library of Congress Control Number: 2012944902

Cover photography by Doug Oldham
www.lightprosystems.com

The Royal Coachman fly tied by Dan and Penny Legere
Maine Guide Fly Shop, Greenville, Maine
www.maineguideflyshop.com

Black & white drawing of the dry fly by Dick Charles.

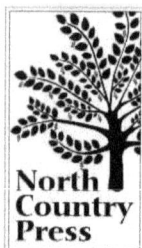

North
Country
Press

Unity, Maine

For Chuck Green, who should not be surprised by this.

Acknowledgments

Every so often, if you live long enough, someone believes in you enough to take a chance on you. I'd like to thank Patricia Newell and North Country Press for taking a chance. I will be forever thankful.

And many thanks to my wife and kids for, well, *everything*.

Foreword

There is a good deal of novelty for me in *Stoneflies and Turtleheads*. It's my first attempt at writing something which *I've* wanted to write. I have written a few articles for trade journals and for some time I wrote gardening pieces for a small Maine newspaper, but at that time my wife and I owned a large nursery business and although writing the column was enjoyable, it was writing I felt I had to do.

Stoneflies and Turtleheads is a collection of essays in which, for better or worse, I try to explain away my lifelong obsession with fly fishing, all while attempting to touch on the sheer beauty of a proper roll cast, of the excitement of a rise, of the love of fishing for a wide variety of fish, of the dedication to the selfishness required in a life of adventure and of the simple romance and poetry of fly fishing. It's a tall order.

Throughout my twenties and thirties, if I wasn't going somewhere I was restless and would feel "off" and not myself. I needed to see the world—to smell it, touch it and try to understand it and as I did, I fished it. I never went anywhere without my SAGE 5-weight fly rod, a single fly box that served as my entire tackle box and a few fly tying tools. I stopped and fished every bit of water I could on four continents and although I was often "skunked" I was never disappointed for I knew then, even as a youngster that I was lucky indeed.

When I look back on two decades of traveling on a shoestring, I realize my idea of adventure may have been a bit askew. It wasn't enough to see the Eiffel Tower, I had to find a couple of the ironworker-maintenance guys and get drunk with them in the Left Bank. It wouldn't do just to see the Wailing Wall, or to touch it...I wanted to dig in the dirt with an archeologist and live for a week with a Jewish family, then with the Bedouin and another week with a Palestinian family. (You would think I would have learned *something*.) In short, I tried like hell to get dirty...to find out what made people in other cultures tick. Along the way, I did find out what made them tick and quite often, from the Middle East to the Arctic and from South America to Europe, I watched people suffer and die, laugh and persevere, and I fell in love more than a few times—with people and places. The only constants I enjoyed were an open mind, my fly rod and the basic goodness that can be found in individuals in all cultures if you stay long enough and get off the beaten path. I felt so awake when traveling in such fashion, and these days the feeling returns every time I stand in a river, and watch as my fly line cuts through the last hour of sunlight, parting the cloud of mayflies ten feet high and somehow lands gently on the water.

Table of Contents

Getting Skunked

Ellsworth, Maine 2009

Getting skunked is not the worst thing in the world. Dealing with it requires perspective and a good attitude. I once watched an older gentleman fish for a couple of hours (don't judge me) down at Grand Lake Stream, landing salmon after salmon. Nymphing, he was. It seemed effortless. Flyfishers to either side of him never hooked-up. Later, in the parking lot, I got to talk to him for a while as he was breaking down his gear. "Have you *ever* been skunked?" I asked. "Once," he said, with a wink..."had to take a bath in tomato juice." Perspective and attitude.

I never really care if I get skunked. Fly fishing is so lovely, so rewarding in itself, it's simply alright to come up empty-handed. It's true. Every fly fishing trip has a raft of rewards one can soak up if you're open minded enough. Like stopping at a hardware store you've never seen before in the middle of nowhere. It's still owned by a local family, still smells the way a hardware store should and it has a neat old well-worn hardwood floor. You stand near the counter while your buddy looks for the duct tape, and you realize that in every direction there is stuff you just can't find anymore. You went in to take a leak and walked out with homemade beaver-jerky, a bottle of pop (because you've never heard of the brand) some pot holders that are mittens made to look like lobster claws and a hard-boiled egg slicer. You get to the truck and think, *this place is great!* and realize you never did hit the head.

You fish hard for the next two days, but it's late in the season and you get skunked and all you remember about the trip is the laughter, the hardware store and how Dave fell out of the car when he stopped for the nineteenth time to off-load some beer. All fishing trips are good trips, unless someone dies. Even then I guess it depends on several contributing factors, like how old or infirm the person is, and if the deceased has been a life-long fly fishing bum or not. All things considered, even with the dying, it could be the best fishing trip ever. I've personally never been on a fatal fly fishing trip...unless you count fish fatalities, of course. Or road-kill.

Just as the journey itself is at least as important and often more interesting than the arriving someplace, fishing trips often become more about the stuff that happens independent of fishing. Things like the meals, the new acquaintances, the drinks, the jokes (often about the flatulence), the stories and the music.

Some years ago my friend, Lloyd Harmon, and I planned a trip to the Arctic. Four of us went in Lloyd's Mooney (a beautiful four-seater airplane) all the way to Baffin Island. Long trips in small planes to difficult places, in true wilderness, with potentially some of the toughest weather in the world, require a certain type of participant. Everyone should be what we in Maine call "good in a tight spot," not too whiny, not too bossy, cheerful in all weathers...that kind of stuff. Old climbing buddy Doug Oldham fits the bill, and so does Lloyd, and so does my Father-in-law Dick Hill, who I think has read everything ever written about the arctic. It was also helpful that Lloyd happens to be a surgeon and a world-class pilot and navigator.

Any trip to the Arctic requires a lot of logistical planning and preparation. Things like flying to Montreal to ship all of our donnage to Iqaluit weeks in advance of the trip, with no specific receiver, hoping all the while that the tents, sleeping bags and other gear will be there when we get there...and hopefully some place where we can find it. Canadians are cursed with an innate sense of kindness, helpfulness and magnanimity. Somehow they haven't let those qualities escape, in spite of our close relationship. With minimal communication, we

3

showed up in Iqaluit many weeks later with only the clothes on our backs. There was our gear, tucked in a hanger at the airport, together, intact, in a nice dry place, looking as though it was cared for. Love the Canadians.

Catching arctic charr was high on the to-do list, but, as usual the trip became more about the culture. Baffin Island, as it turns out is a truly unique place. The Inuit have a very cool (so to speak) culture and Baffin can be absolutely beautiful and foreboding all at once, which usually makes for great adventure. All four of us still feel, years later, that it is one of the best adventures we've been on...and collectively there have been a lot of trips.

As usual we used no travel advisers or agents. The M/O is to do some research, acquire some maps and charts, figure out the fuel access and come up with a plan. Pick out a mountain to climb and come up with an approach. If we're going to need boats, where can we rent them? Unencumbered with competent planning on my part, the guys were wide open for adjustments, which is always best. Lloyd's perfect flight plans were set, but as is so often the case in the arctic, we did have to let the trip evolve as we went along.

I asked a few friends who had fished for charr what flies they used and it seemed that any flashy, bright streamer on a number eight or six long-shank hook would work. I packed the eight weight Orvis and the salt reel and we were ready. There was one other consideration worth mentioning, though. I can't remember if Dick took along a fishing rod or not, but he did take a Ruger #1 .45/70 single shot rifle with a handful of 350 grain bullets. We were going to be camping, remember, in tents...in the arctic. A friend of mine once told me that all kinds of bears will attack or defend themselves in certain conditions, but that polar bears will actually hunt down humans for food. I don't know if that's true or not, but it's sure enough noteworthy. It seems the fishing is often best in places where you need to be concerned with self-defense, or at least your safety.

We eventually found ourselves in the village of Pangnirtung, half-way up Pangnirtung Fiord, a finger of water that juts inland from Davis Straight on the eastern side of Baffin. It was in Pangnirtung that we had to cash in on some of that world-class piloting from Lloyd just getting into town. Pang, as it's called, is my favorite of all Inuit towns I've ever seen. The beautiful surroundings, a genuine wildness, extremely friendly people and its proximity to Auyuittuq National Park makes Pang a popular destination. But the airport landing strip...not so beautiful. I'm not a pilot, but landing there goes something like this: You approach the town by flying above or "up" the fiord, often, as we did, in a thick, zero visibility cloud bank. You decide you're damned sure of your bearings and you drop (Lloyd called it a descent) spiraling down out of the clouds. From wherever you are at that point, you steer the plane towards the town, directly at a cliff. Just before hitting said cliff, you bank ninety degrees to starboard and approach the runway. By runway, of course I mean a short gravel road with a distinct crown in the middle ending abruptly at the edge of the sea. Yeah, that's how I remember it. It's also worth mentioning that Pang is a "dry" town, so even if you do survive the landing, it's hard to celebrate in the appropriate fashion. Substance abuse is well documented in some Inuit villages, and I don't know if I could draw a direct correlation of the lack of alcohol to the pleasantness of Pang, but some of the locals did.

We set up camp just outside of town and set about finding a boat to rent. We were told that the best chance for charr were up one of the smaller fiords that stab into the island from Davis Straight, reaching in from the sea, like fingers trying to get a grip on the land. There are lots of fiords.

The next day we loaded into a homemade plywood boat, about nineteen feet long, owned by local elder Livee Kalualik. His teenage son came along, and his body language told us he would've really rather stayed home and played gameboy. We hired Livee for the day, and I thought maybe his son came along to help us tourists get on-and-off the boat, but it became apparent that he was there to ride shotgun, sitting on the deck of the boat with a .22 magnum rifle, waiting for a seal to pop its head up. He took a lot of shots, and never came close. Dick and I exchanged looks and silently agreed that he was missing on purpose so he wouldn't have to clean the seal when we got back home (dirty business). Apparently, teenagers are the same above the Arctic Circle.

We negotiated dozens of ice floes and bergs as we wound our way up Shark Fiord under an indigo blue sky. The sea was a wonderful teal blue and it contrasted beautifully with the pure white ice. The floes had striations of pastel blues and the patches of grass amongst the granite boulders lining the shore finished the painting perfectly. At the head of the fiord we (or at least *I*) were surprised to see a large Inuit campsite. It was August, and the Inuit for years (maybe thousands) have been semi-nomadic, establishing summer camps along the coast near fresh water close to good hunting and fishing. This was one. The extended family that camped in the grass and rocks was Livee's. They were happy to see us, and greeted Livee in the same way my family would greet my father if his children and grand kids were waiting for him down at camp in Maine. An explosion of color in the earthy landscape, there were the usual bright red, almost orange arctic charr flesh hanging from driftwood racks, kids in Metallica t-shirts, a huge bearded seal skin stretched out on a slab of granite, big white wall tents and lawn chairs set up.

The Inuit have a history of being exploited and treated with disrespect as much as most aboriginal people, but they never lost their fundamental nature, which is dominated by good will. When the early explorers in the nineteenth century beat their way through the passages and straights in search of the elusive Northwest Passage in an effort to find a quicker route to the far side of the world, most of them felt it was beneath them to ask for assistance from the natives.

Many of them thought it would be ridiculous to think those stone-age people could teach them *anything* at all. So for decades, they never learned a thing from the Inuit. They just stood on the decks of their ships, frozen in the ice, wearing their felt boots, woolen coats and long handles. Many of them observed the natives in their sealskin pants, fur coats, boots and mittens. By accounts in their journals, a lot of the same explorers (especially the well-bred officers) thought, "look at those poor, primitive people." Then many of them died. Not the Eskimos...the explorers. In the end, it often wasn't bad seamanship, or lead poisoning from food tins, or lack of toughness that made arctic exploration so dangerous, it was basic prejudice. Of course there were exceptions—men who thrived in the environment, embraced the Inuit and learned from them, but they were in the minority.

The Inuit have always been, and still are, a beautiful culture. They welcome anyone into their homes...just be sure to take off your shoes. It's a big deal with them. They're humble, capable, giving and world-class survivors. The evidence is everywhere on Baffin.

As we unloaded our gear from Livee's boat, three large charr swam lazily by about six feet from shore, maybe thirty inches long each. I couldn't get the rod rigged quick enough.

The idea that day was to walk a mile up the freshwater stream which emptied into the fiord nearby and have an other-worldly fishing experience, catching charr hand over fist, all of them as long as your leg. We made the walk, we fished, and we walked back. I tried every fly I had with me. Nothing. The stream opened up into some very small ponds before it started to run downhill, cascading into little pools where the tide came up to take them over. It was low tide when we were there and we tried casting to some of the pools to no avail. We had come a long way to get skunked. As I said, I don't mind getting skunked. It's just, well...I realized quickly that I had entirely the wrong tackle.

I looked downstream to one of the last pools. There at the base of a huge boulder was Livee's boy with two others about the same age, tossing ten pound charr over their shoulders, one after another. "Great!" I thought. That was my chance to find out what lures were working. I was sure they weren't fly fishing, but I knew if I got a look at what they were fishing with, I could then approximate it with a fly. It took a few minutes to work my way down to them, picking my way through the boulder-strewn field. I was hurrying a bit, excited about the prospect of finally getting a shot at some big fish. My pace softened as I got nearer...from a kind of impatient scurry to a cautious walk, then to a kind of "are you shitting me" halt when I realized the boys were gaffing the fish with homemade gaffs made from hockey sticks and sharpened rebar. They were standing in the pool thigh-deep, in their head-banger rock'n roll T-shirts, thrashing around and scaring the beautiful charr shitless, hooking and tossing them onto the bank. It was disconcerting. You could say I was bummed-out. Not because the boys were gaffing a really cool gamefish...this was their backyard after all. It was just that I really wanted to catch Goddamned charr! Did I mention that it was a long way to go to get skunked? We headed back to the

Kalualik's summer campsite, stopping along the way to check out the many ancient tent rings along the stream, strewn with old, bleached-out bones. Some of the rings were probably hundreds of years old, and it wasn't hard to imagine them covered with driftwood and animal skin tents...little Inuit boogers running around naked in the rare warm summer sun, the older boys down in the stream gaffing charr with sticks and whale-bone hooks, tossing them onto the same section of the stream bank.

We lingered a bit on our way out of shark fiord, stopping to eat lunch and soak-up the warm arctic sun reflecting off of the small ice floe we tied up to, me keeping my eyes open, hoping for some big fish to swim by, Livee watching for some suicidal ring seal to pop up.

Back at our camp outside of Pang, Doug and I prepared ourselves for our attempt on one of the un-named, un-climbed peaks near the end of Pangnirtung Fiord. We made the climb, but this is a tale about the fish. The climb was hard, there was blood, there was soreness, there was beauty and ecstasy, the climbing was wonderfully difficult and there was success. But the *fishing*...that was really hard!

Early on the morning of our last day in Pang, after most of my gear was packed, I took my rod into town. It looked like dead low tide, and I thought that if there was time after checking the weather at the "airport" and one more glance in the Interpretive Center, I might try a few casts from the rocks that poke out of the mud flats near the town dock.

In Maine the tides are pretty fast, and they seem to get quicker the farther north one goes. The Bay of Fundy tides are notoriously fast, and some say they're dangerous, but on Baffin the warnings are everywhere. Signs were posted at the department store in Iqaluit, at the airports, the ATM's...it seemed I couldn't use a restroom without being warned of the imminent tsunami I would experience twice a day. I was worried for a time that I might be overtaken in my sleep. I chalked it up to a slight exaggeration meant for some citified-tourist who might not realize the awesome power omnipresent in nature, but now it was on my mind as I hopped from rock to rock, attempting to get close enough to the water's edge.

When I got out far enough to make a fifty-foot cast meaningful, I picked out a rock big enough to turn around on and, before casting, looked behind me and chose a definitive escape route. (It's always good to have an escape route.) I remember looking at the shore and thinking, "God...that's got to be two hundred yards." As I stripped out some line, I looked down, picked out a small rock in front of me and found on it an indentation that I could use as a reference point. When the water rose to that mark, I'd stop and head for shore. No city boy was I.

A few half-hearted casts along the shore, "uphill" towards the incoming tide from Davis Straight produced nothing. I switched from a Black Ghost to a sparsely tied Nine-Three with a bunch of extra tinsel tied into it, made specifically for this trip. The second cast, and I was fetched. I raised the rod tip gently to be sure, and the line moved sideways. A fish! A small fish, but after so much disappointment at getting skunked days before, my heart jumped. I played it for a moment, then hauled it in aggressively (4x tippet). A small charr...but a fish nonetheless. The hook dislodged, I bent over to release it, and as he (or she) swam away, I knelt for a moment, frozen. The little rock with the indentation was gone...underwater completely. I had been there maybe eight minutes! I knew that I'd have to hurry, and started reeling as fast as I could. As I reeled, I looked behind me, towards shore. I was surrounded by water, maybe shin deep, and some of my escape route was gone. I immediately stopped reeling, stripped in the rest of the line, snapped off the fly and tossed it. I flipped the rest of the line back out through the guides, spun the rod around so that it pointed out behind me and started for shore. The water *was* coming fast. Faster than any tide I'd ever seen. By the time I reached the shore, I was running, slurping through the mud, trying not to lose a boot, the green fly line flying behind me. I tossed the rod off to the side onto the grass then lunged up onto the bank, exhausted. There was probably no real chance of my drowning, but there was every chance of being embarrassed, and I was. As I caught my breath I noticed a couple of locals nearby, the older fellow holding his hand up as if to say "Well, OK, you made it...," and the teenage boy with him pulling their rowboat back up on the rocks. It was obvious they had been watching the show and were getting ready to come get me if I got into any real trouble. The look on the boy's face clearly said, "Damned citified tourist."

I doubt you missed the point. No, we didn't have a great charr-catching experience, but we did have a world-class trip and we all came away with memories still cherished years later. What does the bumper sticker say? "A bad day of fishing is better than a good day at work." Some bumpers are wicked smart.

Notes on Prose and Maine Speak

Maine is an independent state, and Mainers are an independent lot. We have a healthy awareness of, and nervousness of getting too much "help" from away, especially from the federal government. We can sound a little Maine-centric when we call anyone who's not from Maine *from away*, and the term sticks. My daughter was born in Arizona, and we moved back to Maine when she was ten months old. If she lives here in the state until she's 100, she'll still be from away.

We definitely have our quirks, and some of those quirks are regional. For instance, downeast in Washington county the favorite drink is Allen's Coffee Brandy, but the locals call it either "a Downeast panty-dropper" or my favorite, "Fat Ass in a Glass."

We love to make fun of people from Massachusetts in virtually every facet of life (there is a history there) but it's only teasing and we all know someone we love from the Bay State. (We have a favorite nickname for them which we often hurl in their general direction, but only on the road, in traffic, and only with a sort of strange affection...like we didn't really mean it. Mass folks have yet to learn to drive.) We never actually fight, but often needle each other and we never forget we're blood relatives and will rush to the aid of each other in times of need. We like to say things like, "the greatest Red Sox fans in the world live in Maine," just to get them going. We also seem to have a connection with those from Wisconsin and Michigan, but I have no idea why. It is what it is, as they say.

I've heard and read differing theories from sociologists and writers as to why Mainers have embraced their own verbiage and sayings, none of which I put much stock in. It's nothing more complicated than how simple accents develop in different regions. That, and the fact that we have a sophisticated and refined self-effacing sense of humor about ourselves. We have to.

We don't tap things with a hammer...we "*tunk*" them. A little of something is a *dight* (or dite). "Would you like some sugar? Just a dight." Or maybe a *smidgin'*. My aunt Charlotte once told me that *dight* came from an old Dutch penny or something, but she was the same aunt who informed us that her doctor advised her if she tried to quit smoking the shock to her system would kill her.

We often anthropomorphize machinery and equipment (all boats are female, regardless of what the name is) and vice/versa. Like if a woman has a nice butt, we might say, "she's got a nice lower unit," a reference to the business end of an outboard engine. Hey...it's a very important piece of equipment when you have something like 3,000 miles of coastline. Or, "she's a little broad across the beam," referencing the width of a boat amidship.

If we get hurt, we are "*all stove-up,*" or "*all stoved-to-Hell,*" or "*bunged-up.*" (The latter can also mean constipated.) If one is uncoordinated, they are *gommy*. Not sure of the spelling of that one. If such a person just falls down a lot for no apparent reason, they're *wicked gommy*. Or maybe they're prone to fits. If someone gets hysterical, they had a conniption. If someone is unable to cope with pain, they're *spleeny*. But spleeny didn't always mean whimpy...in the old days (we don't say olden days) spleeny meant that you couldn't take the cold weather.

If someone is remarkable, in a funny, clever way we might say, "He's a *rig.*" Steve Martin's a rig. If you take a corner too fast in your pick-up and go into a slide, you might exclaim, "I almost lost my average!" (A train reference.) If the river or stream water is too low to canoe, it's *boney*. Boney can also be used for small brooks, when the water is so low it's not worth fishing because the trout have moved to the ponds, lakes or spring-holes. Boney can also refer to a dirt road in springtime that's "rough going."

You don't accelerate when driving, whether it's a Porsche or a '71 Dodge Powerwagon. You "*give 'er the gas,"* or you *"put the boots to 'er." Put the boots to 'er* has several references. If you're negotiating some big boulder in a particularly boney road, trying to bottom-out on the frame of the car and not the oil pan, someone might say, *"Don't be kittenish with it."* Which means, be serious and don't fool around.

If a specific location is close-by, it's *"a step up the road."* Road is pronounced, *rudd.*

Anything that is big is an "ol' bastid" even if it's brand new. A one year old smallmouth bass of exceptional size is an *ol' bastid.* If you fall down a hill, you "took a tumble" (or a *headah*) even a fatal fall from, say, 300 feet. Example; "How did Linwood die?" "Oh, Mista-man, he took a wicked tumble."

Most people are familiar with the affirmative response, *ayuh.* It's on billboards and everything. Some of the older folks (*old timahs*) will often answer yes with a sudden, short inspiration. Hardly audible. I can't even spell it phonetically. Oh, and it's alright for men to call each other "dear" (pronounced, *deah*) but usually in the workplace. And we don't eat venison, we eat *deah meat.*

The driveway and the yard immediately adjacent to the gravel or hot-top is the *dooryard* (again, don't annunciate either "r"). You might hear *tuther* instead of "the other" as in, "...tuther day while fishin' upta camp I hooked myself in the eeah," or, "We'll get there, one way tuther."

18

In Maine it is perfectly acceptable to have your cat *spaded*. In fact, it's considered responsible pet ownership.

If you are physically so close to an object that you're touching it, you are *"hard-up against it."* Dissimilar objects also. You could be in a doctor's waiting room and hear someone say, "Eban couldn't winch the truck out by himself 'cause a tree was hard up against the front quarter panel...it was a rock maple, three feet at the butt. How he got it stuck like that, I'll never know...he must have been wicked hammered." Hammered, by the way, is pronounced *HAM-id*, but you could also say blitzed, snockered, wasted, shit-faced, stumblin'...the list is long. Mostly because the winters are long.

If a task is particularly difficult, it *"took some doing."* As in, "How the Hell did they move that three story Victorian house from Vinylhaven to the mainland, all in one piece?!" "Took some doing."

I remember some of my father's comments about food. When he would bite into a particularly tough cut of meat (they were *all* particularly tough) he would invariably say, "This is tougher than a boiled owl." If the soup was too hot, he would say "...it's hotter than a two-dollar pistol."

One doesn't dab something (as in paint or glue), one *dobs*. You may say "no" if you want, but if you're emphatic, reply "daow!" You also can say that someone is tough, strong or physically fit, but it's best to say they're *ruggid,* as in "That Dick Butkis is some ruggid."

A fathom in the nautical world is six feet. It is in Maine also, where it can also mean "understand." I may have heard my Dad say to me once, "I can't fathom what's wrong with that boy!" I'll be honest...he said it all the time...but usually he would just shake his head and mumble, "somethin' wrong with that boy."

A tree on its side in the woods is a *blowdown,* unless it has been cut down. If you find it before it gets too *punky,* you can *twitch* it out and cut it up for firewood. Hardwood is best but it might be a *popple* (a poplar).

Little chain ponds which are part of a stream system, or old beaver ponds are often called *bogans.* And speaking of beavers, they live in *houses*...not lodges, whether they know it or not. And we fish for brook trout or *brookies, never* for speckled trout, or "square tails." And some of us will make the drive a couple of times a year for the more rare *blueback* trout. Please don't call them charr (brookies are just as "charr" as bluebacks) or Sunapee trout...which are very close cousins to bluebacks but are NOT the same fish. Call them bluebacks. And it's okay to spell charr with two "rr's",...charr, even in Maine.

If you're trying to get to a bogan and the *pukabrush* is so thick that it's too *hahd goin'*, you might get stopped altogether and get *balled-up*. Balled-up can also mean you're in mid-sentence and got excited, and started to stutter or forget what to say next. Example: "Then Hazen started runnin', and he slammed into a popple and banged his head!! But got up just as the she-bear was bearin' down on him and Deak grabbed him by the shirt and I- he- Oh- then- ah-we-um...Jesus! I'm all balled up!"

It's acceptable to refer to another man as *chummy* or *chummly* or *mista man* or *bub* both in affection or when ready to do battle. It's all in the inflection, so be careful. You might end-up getting a *thrashin*.

There are a few mispronunciations I hear around home these days that I don't think are neat, or cute or endearing...just embarrassing. Instead of foliage, I sometimes hear *foil-age* and it drives me nuts. When cashiers hand me a credit card slip and ask me for my *John Henry*, I cringe, look them straight in the eye and defiantly give them my *John Hancock* instead. I'm probably being passive-aggressive.

There's no way I'll be able to remember all the sayings or strange words I grew-up with, but suffice it to say Maine speech is colorful, different and downright fun. I still enjoy listening when some locals chat, especially after they've had a few *beeahs*. Just for *shits-and-giggles*.

21

Amongst Fishers of Men

(or, Fly Fishing the Holy Land)
Bradley, Maine 2010

Simon Peter saith unto them, I go afishing;
they say unto him, we also go with thee.
JOHN 21:3

My first time to the Holy Land was in 1988 as a
free-lance photographer, working on a book
attempting to cover the first forty years of Israel. I had
a photographic assistant, three Nikon bodies, six
lenses, a Bogan tripod, a notebook, a journal, a tape
recorder, a photographic wish-list, an itinerary
complete with contacts and appointments for
interviews, and, of course, "Sweetness," my 5 weight
Sage fly rod.

I won't pontificate about the spirituality of the
place, or write about how enlightening it is because A:
I'm not smart enough to articulate it, and B: I'm
trying to write essentially about fly fishing, without
too much of life getting in the way...similar to when
I'm actually fishing. If the fishing seems to have

some spirituality in the telling, well, that would make sense and it probably can't be helped. You can't take a deep breath in Israel without feeling the weight of the place, the power of her importance in the world, and the magnificence and romance of the history. And it would also make sense because fly fishing is damned spiritual anyway, no matter where you are.

Some of my friends, who already were aware of my intermittent bouts of transient insanity thought it was odd to take Sweetness to the Middle East. But I explained to them that people have been fishing there for thousands of years, and that it is well known that some of the apostles were fishermen. If you can net a fish, you ought to be able to coax him into taking a fly. I left the nymphs at home and took only a small collection of flies, mostly streamers which in New England I used to fish the salt for mackerel, bunker, sea-run trout and for stripers. I took one reel with a medium-fast sinking saltwater line. I knew that I'd be going from tip-to-tip of the country, which would take me to the Sea of Galilee and to the Red Sea, as well as the Med.

The flight from New York was uneventful, which is good. Any "event" on an international flight is usually negative (with one important exception). El Al Airlines wasn't great...it was cramped, and during a trip to the head, it appeared as though they had unbolted and then moved each row of seats forward, so they could add a couple of rows at the back of the plane. When we finally landed in Tel Aviv, a design from the fabric in the seat in front of me was deeply imprinted into my knees and stayed there until I left the pub two hours later.

The fishing didn't come quick. I did have a job to do, and the first night was spent in Jerusalem, going over side trips and appointments over the next few weeks. There was an interview with a Nobelist, photograph the synagogue at Hadassah Hebrew Medical Center, a trip to the Church of the Holy Sepulchre, and then a trek across a good portion of the Negev in southern Israel. Pretty heady stuff. Before the desert trek, we would go to the port city of Eilat, at the northern tip of the Red Sea—my first chance to wet a line. After that, it would be the Dead Sea, the ruins of Ashkelon, Masada, the West Bank...you get the picture.

After about a week of taking care of business, we finally made our way south to the port city of Eilat at the northern tip of the Red Sea. As it turned out, the most interesting part about Eilat wasn't the city so much as our contact there, Shmulik Marco. Marco at the time was the local director of the Field School of the Society for Protection of Nature in Israel (SPNI). Part Sierra Club, part boy and girl scouts and part Nature Conservancy, the SPNI is pretty amazing. Like many such organizations, it was born of a response to that old scourge of the earth—developers. The SPNI probably wouldn't make a statement as politically incorrect, but I will. In 1953 a group of teachers and scientists got together to protest the draining of the Hula swamplands to the north. It was the first time any such action was taken to preserve the delicate environment of Israel. The SPNI evolved into field schools where the public could be educated about nature. They've even taken the government to court. (Some governments are careful with the environment...others, not so much. Remember, Israel was young then and had a unique set of concerns surrounding them. Nowadays they're pretty careful.) Marco, tall, lean and super intelligent, was in Eilat to ensure the evolution continues. When I was last in Israel in 1990, even the military was working closely with SPNI. When the military wanted to build a new base in a sensitive area, they would call the Society. The Israeli Defense Forces even worked with the SPNI regarding bird migration routes, work that not only saved bird lives, but cut down on bird strikes, which pilots apparently hate.

Schmulik was kind enough to show me the best places for bird watching (a big deal in Eilat), the only spots he could think of for fly fishing, and helped map out my upcoming trek through the Negev. Over our evening meal on the first night, he explained the essence of the Field School (we billeted in the school's dormitory) and I was so taken by the selflessness of the organizers that for years I made small charitable contributions. I would be still if I had any money. It's easy to agree with things like "awareness and knowledge of the natural environment" and "...outings to stimulate large numbers of people to deepen their attachment and involvement."

When I got the chance over the next few days while still in Eilat, I tried throwing a fly a couple of times. Once was in an area which seemed to be the absolute northern tip of the sea, among some reeds in a rather industrial section. I tried a maribou muddler minnow, a small nine-three and another streamer with no name which I tied that morning in my room. The day before, while touring the city, I thought I caught a glimpse of a rise or two just off from the reeds, and I might have, but was skunked there. The next day I tried casting from shore across the street from the Field School and went fishless again. There are fish there. I know because there is a sport-fishing industry in the Red Sea, and also because we had snorkeled in the same spot the day before and there were fish everywhere about forty feet from shore. I would have traded in the Mickey-Finn for a spear gun.

It would be a while before I would fish again. The hike across the Negev took seven days because I took some time to explore some of the ancient mines that dotted the hillsides. Another delay came when I spotted some travelers about a half-mile off in a shallow canyon. I could see through the 400 mm lens they were, I believed, Bedouin. I had no idea why, but they made me nervous. I would certainly have been an alien to them, out there in the middle of nowhere with my Lowe backpack and Merrill hiking boots, or maybe not an alien, but rather a lost moron, out of my element (I was actually exactly *in* my element). I gave them a wide berth and went on my way, but the detour cost me a day. It's funny, in retrospect. I don't know what I thought they would do to me, or even why I thought they might harm me, but subsequently over my time in the Middle East my ignorance became painfully obvious. Later, I was allowed to stay with a family in their tent for a week, a few miles east of Jerusalem, and I learned to love the Bedouin. Their hospitality was and is world-class, and they're remarkable survivors. In contrast to the sometimes tenuous allegiance Israeli Arabs show for their state, the Bedouin hold a long record of loyalty. They even patrolled the Jordanian border for the IDF on occasion.

Deeply religious Muslims and tradition-bound, the Bedouin have faced remarkable social changes that have taken place in Israel by employing their greatest inherent trait...survivability. Just fifty years ago, they couldn't conceive of schooling. Children eight years old were valuable workers. Now they wish their children to be educated. Changing abruptly has been tough for them for all the obvious reasons, as I was reminded several times on that trip, "...we're not immigrants."

I've been to many deserts throughout the world, but that hike in the Negev is still one of my favorites. There were wanderers to negotiate, water to ration, tough terrain, torn shoes, and an honest to goodness oasis...just like in the movies, except without the part where an Arab sheik rides up and lops my head off for drinking his water. There was sand, water, rocks, shade, and a few birds. It was only a six-night hike, but that was plenty of time to explore ancient mines, sift through the remains of old campsites and to just sit and stare at the indigo-blue skies. I'd like to have spent a lot more time in the Negev and I remember thinking it would've been perfect if there were a trout stream running through it. But if there was, there would be fly shops and sporting camps. Nice, but no longer the Negev.

Long drives in foreign lands can be a lot of fun, but there aren't any in Israel. Not long after leaving Eilat we found our way to the ruins of Ashkelon in the northern tip of Gaza. It took an hour to find Lawrence Stager, the American professor from Harvard who was supervising the excavation. There were lots of cool archaeological aspects of Ashkelon, like the amazing dog cemetery (look it up) or the pornographic lampshades from the Roman bath houses, but the most unique was the fact that seven different civilizations are buried there, including the Greeks, Philistines, Romans and Crusaders. Of all the coastal cities south of Jaffa, Ashkelon was the only port occupying one of the few coastal combinations of fertile soil and sweet ground water on the Mediterranean, which made for an economy based on agriculture, commerce and shipping.

After an extensive tour of the dig and lots and lots of lampshade photographs, we had lunch with the professor and the students in the shade of some olive pomegranate trees. I snuck away and fetched Sweetness from the rental car and then picked my way through the dig, past the dog cemetery, through the maze of holes (being careful to not step on the string grids laid out everywhere) and then punched my way down through the wild rose brambles to the beach. I had to slide down the bank (holding Sweetness high over my head) between two huge Roman columns. I assumed they were once vertical, holding up a roof or a facade maybe forty feet high. Erosion and time had done its thing and there were several of them now, sticking out of the embankment at various angles, pointing out to sea like cannon still protecting a city that's long gone.

I only had about a half-hour, so I rigged up a long-shank pink lady streamer which is a good attractor fly pattern. I put on the Teva sandals and waded out to some rocks sticking out from the middle of a small beach. I had an old Billy Pate saltwater reel with me which was a little heavy and a bit of a strain on the 5 weight rod, but I could kick out quite a bit of line. I tried casting straight out at first and had no strikes. Casting almost parallel to the shoreline, I caught a few small mackerel, to my surprise, almost at my feet. Before I landed one, I could see them chasing the streamer, three or four at a time. I couldn't be positive what they were until I landed one, but it was fun to feel that old familiar feeling when the heart starts to jump, knowing you've got some fish interested in your fly. They looked exactly like the mackerel I was used to catching off the docks and bridges back in Maine, with their iridescent green backs and the absolutely white bellies.

The tide was on its way in, and soon I would have no place to stand, so I headed back up the hill to the dig. I stopped for a minute to rub my hand gently along one of the Roman columns. I'm not sure why I didn't think about the Roman masons, or slaves, that cut the column, but rather wondered about the Crusaders who passed through them on their way to Jerusalem. Were the columns still standing at that time? Were the streets busy with merchants, soldiers, politicians and prostitutes? Did the air stink from the open sewers, or was someone constantly burning incense in the doorways from plants harvested from the fields in the north? A few more steps and I was struck by how powerful the scent was from the wild roses. Hot pink and beautiful, my mother would have loved them. I had seen farmers in Oman grow roses that looked just like these and harvested the flowers to make rose water, which was like gold to them. Nobody knows who brought the plants to Oman 4,000 years ago. With so much humanity passing through Ashkelon, did someone drop off some seedlings on their way to Mecca, or perhaps England? Maybe there was a Johnny Appleseed type way back when (Saladin Roseseed)? I picked one flower to press in my journal to give to mother and scrambled back to the top of the embankment. As I passed through the dig I saw Dr. Stager and he called to me. I asked him about the Roman columns and he said they were re-used by Muslim rulers in the Middle Ages to strengthen the on-going construction of the day, like giant rebar. Waves have gradually washed away ruins along the shoreline, exposing them. As we walked he showed me an inscription over a wall of a plaster-lined pool in a bath house translated as "Enter, Enjoy, and Screw." He looked at it and said half sadly, half-jokingly, "after all my life's work, I hope this isn't my contribution to science."

I gave the rose I picked that day to mother (who was very religious) and she seemed to like it. She held onto it and would take it out from time to time and ask about the places I visited in Israel. She passed away some years later and I made that flower part of her burial. It meant a lot to me. It seems when someone close to us dies, we will find little things to cling to in an effort to assuage the anguish.

We left Ashkelon and after a few days of conducting interviews in Jerusalem, we took a long route to Galilee. We stopped at another important archaeologic site on the coast about fifteen miles south of Haifa. Brilliant algae covers the old natural breakwaters off the ancient Phoenician port city of Dor. The breakwaters protected the harbor and now Dor is the site of ongoing underwater and land excavations. Large quantities of artifacts have been found dating from Phoenician times through the Napoleonic wars. From the coast road I could see a lone fisherman out on the breakwater surf casting. That's all I needed.

Walking along the lava-like rocky outcropping above the breakwaters, I was sure to hold the fly rod pointing out in back of me in case I stumbled. Once below, the breakwaters were easier to negotiate than they looked from above and the fellow fisherman, who looked shocked to see me (there were no buildings in sight, and very little traffic), smiled and nodded to let me know that it was alright to approach. We spoke briefly. He was fishing for mackerel with what looked to be a fifteen foot surf casting rod. He had a burlap creel which he wore around his waist like a backwards fanny-pack and wore a straw cowboy hat. It was high tide and he had six good sized fish. He said he was catching them for a cook-out that evening, his name was Stef and when he told me he had lived in New York City for a while, I cringed and replied "I'm sorry," as if I really was. He laughed at that, and when I told him I was originally from Maine he brightened-up and said he went on holiday to Ogunquit Beach once. This time I actually *was* sorry. For bait he used a thin sliver of belly cut from the previous fish on a hook, preceded on the leader by two flip-tops from beer cans. They were tied on with a homemade swivel-type thing and functioned perfectly as spinners. I meant to ask him what he baited the first hook with before he had a belly to cut, but forgot.

I asked him if I could try to contribute to his cook-out, for which he was happy. It seemed that he was just happy to have someone to fish with. It's often the same scene the world over.

Having had luck in Ashkelon a few days earlier, I tied on the exact same fly I had used there. I stepped to his right far enough to be out of his way and we fished. The water looked perfect for surf fishing there, and it was. I actually could cast out farther with the Sage than he and caught a mackerel on the first cast. It seemed like the schools were swimming up and down the shoreline, or maybe in-and-out with the waves, but I picked one up with about every forth cast. I saw Stef watching me intently, and I asked if he'd like to try the fly rod. He had that "you're reading my mind" look and I gave him a quick casting lesson. I swear within six tries he was casting without breaking his wrist at all and was almost patient enough on the back cast. It was enough to get plenty of line out. He caught two or three and was like a kid in a candy shop. He told me what little he knew about the ruins directly behind us, about his home and about how swimmers at the beach to our left had been getting stung on the foot by "weever fish" recently.

He said the weever fish have no swim bladder, so when they stop swimming they sink to the sandy bottom; half burying themselves in the sand, ambushing shrimp and small fish as they swim by. He told me the sting is horrible, and shared tales of sailors that had been stung who would cut off their fingers to relieve the pain. I was fascinated, but I caught myself thinking "maybe a Joe's Smelt would work."

I told him I had to go and gave him the fish I caught for his cook-out. He implored me to stay and be his guest that night with his family, and although that's the kind of thing I live for when traveling, I declined and explained that I had an appointment at Galilee in the morning. He asked for some advice about flyrods and I told him that many companies offer starter outfits for beginners, I told him LL Bean is set-up pretty well for shipping internationally, and the lifetime guarantee would be hard to beat. I had fished with him for an hour and it felt as if we had fished together for years. We shook hands, then hugged goodbye and as I climbed up the rough rocks to the road, picking my way through the yellow coreopsis, I knew we had another fly fisherman in the world—in Israel, no less.

The Sea of Galilee is a lake by any other name. Actually, a bunch of other names...Lake Tiberias, Sea of Tiberias, Lake Kinneret, Lake Gennesaret, Sea of Chinneroth, Bahr Tubariya, and others. Like opinions and ideas in Israel, it depends who you talk to. I only heard Israelis refer to it as Lake Kinneret, in fact they often referred to the surrounding area as "The Kinneret." We stayed at a couple of kibbutzim while I photographed the eastern shore and the Golan foothills.

In contrast to the dry desert environment of much of central and southern Israel, the north and east, especially the Golan Heights, are beautifully lush and fertile. Lake Kinneret, surrounded by papyrus bushes, palm and olive trees, is the only sweet-water lake in the region. It feeds vast farmlands in the arid Negev through a system of pipes, canals and pumps which spread out to much of the coastal plain. I photographed the target list from the editors and on the second night, I finally got to cast a line on the shore. Earlier in the day, I spoke with a local fisherman named Itamar, while he sorted out his nets and I poked-around for some local knowledge as fishermen often do.

Staying for four days at a farm cooperative on the beautiful shore of the Sea of Gallilee, learning about the working of the kibbutz, eating healthy and, best of all, fishing the lake in the evenings, was paradise found. Fed by underground springs, the main source of the lake is the Jordan River, which flows through it from north to south. The lake lies low in the Jordan Great Rift Valley and is surrounded by hills, and is prone to sudden violent storms (as in: New Testament story about Jesus calming the storm). Everybody warned me when I borrowed a small boat on the second day. I tried to explain that I cut my watercraft teeth on certain lakes back home (Moosehead, West Grand...) but was dismissed. Everything that happens in the Holy Land has more import—even storms...whether romantic, political, or climatic. I found the water quite benign in that little punt, but on the very next day I was photographing windsurfers when a Hell of a storm came up from the west and drove every vessel off the lake and us inside.

There's an absolute poetry to fly fishing that surely doesn't exist in any other method of catching fish. It is a natural, primal poetry that doesn't show up very often in sports...maybe even in life. It's hard to convey how special it was to be a part of that poetry (the fisherman is by far the least important component in the poetic device) there on the shores of Galilee, where much of the ministry of Jesus Christ occurred. In the days when Christ walked the earth, there was a continuous development of settlements around the lake. The gospels of Matthew and Mark tell us how Jesus recruited four of his apostles from the shores; Peter, Andrew, John and James. A lot of heady stuff went on there...His walking on water, calming a storm, feeding 5,000 people, and other miracles I can't remember from Catechism. So yeah, fishing from the same shores felt...more important.

The primary fish in the Sea of Galilee is Tilapia, known locally as "St. Peter's Fish." I caught them every evening about thirty feet from shore. The later the evening, the closer they came to the reeds in shallower water along the shore. The moniker "St. Peter's fish," comes from the Christian story about the apostle Peter catching a fish with a coin in its mouth. The passage doesn't name the fish, but it *was* in the Sea of Galilee, so, Tilapia it is.

There are dozens of species of cichlid fish from the tilapiine tribe. I know they exist on at least four continents. They thrive in just about any freshwater habitat as long as the water temperature never gets below 50 degrees Fahrenheit. The varieties I've caught always remind me of a red-eyed cross between a funky perch and a bass. They eat just about anything, but they're primarily herbivores, eating floating and submerged plants and most forms of algae. We lived in

Arizona for a few years, and I would often catch them in the canals around Phoenix. That state stocked tilapia in an effort to control the algae and to help purify the water. Little #18 elk hair caddis flies don't look like any plants I know, but in those canals I found the tilapia would take them eagerly.

The first evening at the kibbutz I tied on the only caddis I had with me. In fact, it was the only dry fly in my box. I had figured on just streamer fishing on the trip. First cast, I snagged a reed in my back cast and broke it off. I ran back to the room and gathered up my vice and bobbin. There were some goats wandering around the kibbutz, and yes, I did ask permission. We quickly tied some goat hair caddis flies. We all took turns catching (and harvesting) eight-inch Tilapia until after dark. It never took more than three casts to hook one. There were no coins. I checked them all.

On that particular trip, it wasn't the fishing I remember the most; it was the people and the place. I find it interesting that on a trip filled with interviews with world-class individuals, dinners, contacts and meetings, it was while fishing I made the most meaningful connections with local people. No wonder Jesus would hang out with so many fishermen.

One colossal bummer about the trip was that I didn't get to fish the Jordan River. On the day we left Galilee, heading back to Jerusalem, I photographed some hikers near the Jordanian border as they paralleled the River. It was almost treeless except along the banks, with beautiful tall green grasses, more yellow coreopsis and the occasional blooming almond tree, which looked like a stunning cross between a cherry tree and an apple tree in bloom. The hikers, in single file along the dirt path winding through the perfect green landscape, reminded me of the Ecuadorian highlands. I only had time to scoot down to the river's edge while the hikers took a water break. They were a group from a nearby kibbutz. One hiker said there was a kibbutz near theirs which raised rainbow trout. Quite often, the farmed fish escaped into the river. Over time there has been a sustained population in certain sections of the River Jordan. I told her I fly fished and that I was a little late now for Jerusalem, so there was no time to fish. As I glared into the rolling, perfect pocket water, she could see that her words were killing me - rainbows in the Jordan. I don't know what she knew of the life of a fly fishing bum, but she said, "It's hurting you isn't it?" Normally, that would be an understatement, but not in that place, on that day.

And the goat hair caddis fly? I had it for years before I misplaced it. I wish I still had it. To bury with one of my fly fishing buddies who thought it was ridiculous and teased me about it. *After* he's dead, of course.

Turtlehead

Blue Hill 2007

I was raised within sound and smell of Bass Park in Bangor. The park is still the site of the annual Bangor State Fair (which in my childhood was still a real agricultural fair) and a half mile harness racing track. Beyond the park, to the southwest, was the municipal golf course, and beyond *that* were the Maine Central Railroad tracks coming and going, to and from the west. For generations railroad tracks played an important part in the lives of young boys. They were a quick escape route for youngsters trying to leave home behind, if only for an afternoon. The tracks represented a direct line to Boston, Chicago, the West...they represented a chance for someplace else, for *anyplace* else. A quick walk down the tracks from any part of town, and one was, it seemed, out of town; once clear of backyards and the watchful eyes of neighborhood Moms, railroad tracks could be downright enchanting. Today the escape comes in other forms...Gameboys, computers and iPods.

I was about six when my Father started taking me on Sunday walks the mile or so from home to the railroad tracks. We would strike off out Webster Avenue, past the golf course, cut through the tall pines at the end of the street, beat our way through the blackberry bushes (which Dad called brambles), to a little brook that ran along the tracks and then under the tracks, and emptied into a small "pond" called Turtlehead. It was not a pond at all, but rather a large pool where the brook dumped from the culvert and took a turn to the left on its way to the Penobscot.

There was a second, smaller tributary that drained a cow pasture on the far side of the pond from the Perry farm, which was across the Hampden town line. Always brown and muddy, it served as the cows' watering hole for the Perrys. (In retrospect, I suppose it was just a cow pond.) Pretty ugly at certain times of the year, Turtlehead for me was pure delight because it came to me with such a history attached, and eventually turned mystical along the way. The brook was also referred to as Turtlehead Brook by some, but not by us...the name applied just to the pond.

In 1929, as Trotsky was getting the boot from the Soviet pecking order, another event occurred with a splash at Turtlehead. My Dad learned to swim—the hard way. There were seven boys in his family, and it took three to throw him into the pool. Well over his head, he said "once I finally made it to shore we settled up."

Father enjoyed telling the stories of his youth and, almost always funny, the stories were lousy with history, which I loved.

On more than one occasion, we stopped near the golf course parking lot which overlooked the southwest end of Bangor and across the Penobscot to Brewer. He pointed to where the corn, potatoes and other crops were grown by the Bangor City Farm—now the first, second, third, and fourth holes, and the driving range of the golf course. The farm house itself would later become Beal College. He explained how the city farm worked; how when a family or individual became so far in debt, they were susceptible to being forced into the Alms House (which was the "Farm House"). The inmates (they were actually called that), were required to work the farm if they were able, otherwise they helped out in the house. This was heady stuff for a small child, for suddenly my mother's daily admonishments turned plausible. When we were growing up, *everything* we did had the potential to ruin us as a family unit. No matter whether we broke a neighbor's window, trampled someone's garden or even looked disparagingly at a stranger, someone was inevitably going "...to sue us and we're going to lose the house!" It was common knowledge that we subsequently would be headed for "the Poor House." We kids would roll our eyes.

As incredible as it seemed to me then, maybe Mum was right...perhaps people could pluck us out of our beds and throw us into the Poor House, maybe even separate us. Suddenly the odd notion of empathy was thrust upon me, (I didn't know what empathy was, so remote a notion to a child).

Years later I researched to see if there really was an Alms House. I checked 1919, the year my father was born. Sure enough, I found an annual report from that year. The superintendent and assistant, Mr. and Mrs. Lewis Klatt, reported that in addition to a head farmer and a matron, there were two teamsters, a nurse and two cooks. The house was four stories and contained inmates' quarters, a kitchen, a dining room, two living rooms, and fifty-four sleeping rooms. The number of beds was about seventy-five.

The heading on the report was Hospital and House of Corrections, but was referred to throughout the report as the Alms House. Mr. Klatt noted there was a section of the house devoted to the sick, but the house was primarily for corrections. The superintendent believed there was no good reason the city should separate the sick from the "debtors, drunks and streetwalkers." He reported the cleanliness was very good. Sanitation and care of food supplies was good, although some of the toilets needed replacing.

Discipline seemed kindly. He noted that many of the inmates were very old and could do little. "Some wash dishes, one mends underwear and two keep the wood to the furnace" he wrote.

Catholics seemed to have dropped the ball in 1919...Mass was held twice a year, while the Protestants had a service every Sunday afternoon. As a recovering Catholic myself, I was disappointed with that.

The men and women were segregated, no matter if they were husband and wife. The children went to a juvenile facility on the far side of town, or stayed with relatives if there were any.

The farm produced nearly all of the food for the Alms House—how efficient by today's municipal standards. Here's the kicker: during the growing season, the farm grew enough excess food to sell twice a week, setting up a horse cart at Pickering Square. In the 1918 season, they sold 1,200 bushels of corn, 2 ton of squash, 214 bushels of tomatoes (they grew Brandywine), 66 half-pecks of beans, 980 pounds of onions, and 814 barrels of potatoes (green mountain and Kennebecs). It gets better. All of the non-storage market produce that didn't sell by the end of the day was driven up State Street and donated to Bangor General Hospital. The market helped pay for utilities and for the wages of the matron and the nurse.

Mr. Klatt's chief recommendation that year was to "add a strong woman to the payroll," but he didn't specify for what, at least not in writing.

Beyond the golf course, Dad and I would cross the Perry Road. In those days the only major building nearby was the Cole's Express business, but there were two foundations of farm houses near the road. We would cut through the woods at the end of Cole's parking lot until we hit the brook below the railroad tracks. Our usual trip would follow the brook downstream to Turtlehead, then we'd head home after lunch.

The brook was four to twelve feet wide and about two to four feet deep. It had a mud bottom, very little gravel or boulders. It wasn't fast flowing, but moved quick enough to keep the water oxygenated, and cool enough to hold brook trout? Dad doubted it, but it was fun to pretend. We never carried fishing poles to Turtlehead, but would usually cut a piece of alder and tie on some twine. I always took along some small fish hooks just in case. We also never took worms...instead we would "grub around" and search for, well, grubs.

There were a couple of deep sections of the brook at the tail end of short runs of quick water that always looked fishy. If we were lucky we would catch a couple of chubs. They were big minnows, really, only about 5 inches long.

I only recall one time that you could say we possibly got into any real fish. In late spring one year, while my father started the tiny twig fire to burn the usual hot dogs, I worked my way downstream, got low, and bulled my way through some thickets at the end of the pool. It was so thick, we always walked around that particular puckabrush. When I did pop out at the brook again, I found a new short section of quick water—a little run about three feet deep and nearly twenty-five feet long. It was heavy with brush overhanging the banks. At the far end was an old tree limb down, half in, half out of the water at the end of the bend in the brook. It disturbed the flow just enough, and there was a small amount of white foam accumulated just in front of the sticks, spiraling around in a little vortex.

The only bug I had found was a grub, or something that looked more like a brown caterpillar. I impaled it on the hook lengthwise, and not too close to either end, and tossed it into the deepest water in the run (if it could be called that), and nothing. I inched my way downstream toward the foam, stepped into the water twice and got close enough to toss in the grub. It hardly hit the water and there was a flash of a fish. I jerked too quickly and he was gone. I plopped it in again and this time got a good look at him. Not only did he act different than the chubs always did, he had the tell-tale, worm-like lines above his head and down his back...a trout! I couldn't believe it! Hell, I wasn't even thinking about trout—just hoping to catch a chub. In an instant, the fish was gone and so was the grub. I ran back and told Dad everything. I could see in his face there was doubt.

After lunch he carefully dowsed the fire and gave me the umpteenth lecture about how important that was. We went to the spot where I almost hooked "the Big One" and he said, "well, it *is* trouty." He could tell, I think, that his skepticism made me feel bad. Later, when we took a break at the edge of Turtlehead, he told me about how years before, he had stopped on the side of the road where Cold Stream passes under Cold Brook Road less than a mile from where we sat. He spoke of how muddy the water was, and how he didn't think any trout could live there. He tossed in the rig he always used...a swivel followed by a small spinner and a snelled hook on a six-inch leader, with a worm on it—garden hackle. He caught six fat trout! All were keepers, and all six fish, flashing out of the murkiness, hitting the worm hard as though they hadn't fed for weeks. I felt better. (Dad was a meat fisherman, and in those days "catch and release" meant you just caught a neighborhood kid in your rhubarb patch.)

As I got older, I tried that spot many times, hoping to land just one trout for proof. I never hooked one—a few chubs now and again and the occasional eel. The brook was always changing with small deviations in its course and the muddiness of the water. It wasn't from erosion, but from development. Now it's an industrial park.

Turtlehead still is there, but the cows are not. I went back to revisit the old haunt a few years ago. It might have been my imagination (which is vast and tends to wander) but the water seemed clearer. I didn't fish. I went there to be with Dad, who had passed away a few days before. I tried to remember everything he talked about. I thought of when he showed me old hearths and nails in trees near the brook where we fished that day—nails the hobos left during the Great Depression. Some of the nails still had remnants of rotted rope dangling from where the itinerants dried their clothes or hung tarpaulins. He told me about when he was just a kid, two of his brothers and he would sneak over there on summer days (in direct violation of his mother's orders) and visit "Hobo Village." Sometimes, if they "looked alright," the boys would even sit and talk with the folks. I sat on the grassy bank and remembered him telling me, as he stared down at an old cook pot half stuck in the ground, "...life was hard then." An understatement, I suppose. He told me about his father at the tail-end of the Depression. Also a railroad man, he was coupled between two trains and eviscerated and was unable to work for a year. He had many subsequent abdominal surgeries. "There was no such thing as workers comp in those days," he said. With eight kids at home, he lamented, "We found out who our friends were that year."

Whenever a train went by we would wave to the engineer, who always waved back...especially if they recognized Dad—a fellow engineer for the Maine Central.

There were countless trips to Turtlehead with friends; exploring, hunting rabbits with homemade bows and arrows (never got one) and lolling the days away. It was on the opposite side of the tracks from the pond that I shot Dennis Hamel in the lip with a BB gun. It wasn't a miss-fire...we were shooting *at* each other (I never said we were gifted kids). It was the first time we drew blood...and the last BB gun fight. I felt horrible about it. I ought to mention it was a ricochet—I wasn't actually aiming at his head. The rules were to aim below the nipple-line...but some people's nipples are lower than others. Dennis instantly forgave me, as I would have him. I also should mention that he was an exceptionally tough kid. He went on in life to become a generously decorated U.S. Special Forces Ranger, back in the days when it meant something extraordinary to have earned a black beret.

Many years after his retirement from the army the BB is still there, lodged in his upper lip, an occasional reminder of the happy slopes of long ago. A mutual friend told me he had seen Dennis a while back, and the old soldier told him how he had forgotten all about the BB incident. How some years ago he was in Walter Reed or someplace getting prepped for a mission, and how the doctors found this artifact on an x-ray and thought maybe it was a tiny piece of shrapnel. He said "no...I'd remember that." He and the doctors could not figure out what it was. He told our buddy how the medical staff was pondering their next move when Dennis suddenly sat bolt upright in the examination chair and exclaimed, "FUCKING DAUPHINEE!!!!." I guess he remembered after all. When our friend told me the tale, it occurred to me Dennis learned to fight, and I never did...I hope he still forgives me.

As I said, I felt horrible about it. But...when I stop to think...here's a highly decorated Special Forces guy who has been badly injured, but never took a bullet. That means I'm the only one who ever shot him. Pretty cool. Memories? Yeah, there are memories at Turtlehead—mine, my Dad's, his brother's, my friend's, and probably many folks from past generations who I'll never know.

As I sat there, in the same spot where we always cooked lunch when we ate at the pond, I couldn't help but get a little melancholic seeing how much the landscape had changed. Like I said, the cows are gone. They were a pain in the ass back in the day, ruining the water as we tried to fish. But now I missed them. The big pasture that sloped down to the pond had been graded flat, and now there's a road and a parking lot for some kind of business. Some of the trees on the far side of the pond were still there, only bigger. The big granite culvert was the same. The tracks were the same, though it looked like they weren't being used.

It occurred to me then, after several generations of my family playing there, I had never taken my son. Could it be true? We lived in Arizona for some of his childhood, but we've been back in Maine for several years. He's thirteen now, and a pretty sophisticated fly fisherman for his age. I'll take him in the spring. Is the water really clearer than in the old days? Should I break with tradition and take along a fly rod? I don't know...maybe a nymph, no, probably a leach pattern. Then another thing occurred to me, like it did to Dad forty years ago. I should know better than anyone...it doesn't matter one bit if he catches a fish or not.

Maybe I'll tell the boy about the time I fell through the ice one winter, and how Dad built a big fire to dry out my clothes and to warm me up, and how worried he looked. But as worried as he seemed, he joked for years afterward with people how he tried to "...lose him in the ice over to Turtlehead...but damned if he didn't make it home."

Nowadays, access to Turtlehead is too easy. No more long Sunday walks. One only has to drive to a nearby parking lot in the old cow pasture and it feels a little like trespassing. Maybe it is. Maybe they'll sue us and we'll lose the house.

Influences

Concord, New Hampshire 2011

I cringed at the word "hero" as a youngster, but I certainly had people I admired and looked up to. My parents, of course, for making do in a world class way, never complaining and keeping all eight of us kids from killing each other. I had a pretty romantic view of life, and it was Bill Tillman and Eric Shipton who I admired from my books. In Bangor, there was a granola-eating, Willy's driving, middle school art teacher named Mr. Sands who I thought was the bee's knees. My memory isn't clear that far back, but I think he fly fished.

From about the age of ten to thirteen, I was infatuated with my Uncle Ed from Hampden, Maine who was wounded at Anzio (and two other times) and somehow ended-up with Patton in France. He came home from WWII with lots of German military souvenirs. I asked too many questions about the war, as kids often do, and he answered all of them with, "I just pray to God, my boy, that you never know what it's like." He was an actual real-life hero, but according to my aunt, was haunted by the war for the rest of his life.

My own father was pretty amazing as well. I swear, he never did the "wrong thing," he could fix anything and he built our house himself. (Though, as I understand it, he built the house first and then dug the cellar out from under it by hand...I guess they needed shelter first, then plumbing and duct work later as they could afford it. It was a wonderfully simpler time.) Best of all, he knew a great deal about the woods...where most of my interests were.

We fished a lot every summer, and I have more fond memories of our times in the outdoors than I can count. Like the time he was laying on his back under the old Chevy tying up the exhaust pipe with baling wire and I snuck close enough to him to tie his shoe laces together. When he slid out from under the car he (a big man) physically couldn't get up. He had the mastery of emotions to simultaneously curse me and laugh hard, especially when I couldn't stop giggling as I untied them for him. I'm digressing here. We hunted and hiked a lot, but when I daydream about the sunny slopes of long ago, I remember the fishing trips the best.

Dad was a bait fisherman and primarily used worms, and by primarily I mean always. I never saw him use anything other than a small swivel at the end of his monofilament line, then a small spinner of some sort, followed by a #8 snelled hook which came attached to a six-inch leader. He always caught trout, but would sometimes fish for the numerous white perch that were in our lake at camp (for my mother's chowder), and like many of his contemporaries, *never* fished for bass. If he was somewhere and caught a smallmouth accidentally, he would kill it by either wacking its head on the gunwale or simply tossing it onto the bank, too far for it to flip its way back into the water. Bass were "rough" fish and didn't really belong in Maine. I think he felt a bit guilty because smallmouths were seen as intruders in those days and it was his beloved railroad men (Dad was a railroad man), who came before him, that helped in the distribution of the foreign species, dumping buckets of bass into warm water ponds on some of their stops.

Another thing...he never said it, but I think he may have thought fishermen who fly fished were a little snobby. He was definitely a meat fisherman.

I'm in my early fifties now and quickly approaching the old fogey stage of life. I still think long and hard about the endless summer days with Dad on Mopang Stream, Southwest Brook, the Machias River and lots of small, nameless brooks throughout Washington County, dunking worms, getting black-fly bit, stopping to dump the painful pebbles out of my wading sneakers, and opening my creel every five minutes to admire the pretty brookie lying on the ferns at the bottom. The memories are perfect and I cherish them still.

It amazes me now to think back on how much my father knew about fish biology and entomology—a man who only fished with worms. But he taught me a lot and the lessons served me well. They still do.

Enter the Bangor naturalist and writer Bill Geagan. My favorite book as a boy was *My Side of the Mountain* by Jean George. After reading it for the first time during my ninth winter, I became obsessed with the notion of living on my own in the woods, surviving by my own wits. The problem was, I didn't *have* any wits, and my father knew it. After a few weeks of badgering him to let me try, he finally said, "Okay, Bill Geagan from the Bangor Daily knows something about this sort of thing, let's talk to him and see what he thinks about it." Bill and Dad were acquaintances, and we saw him every Sunday at church. After Mass the next week, we both approached Mr. Geagan and his wife Alice. Dad introduced me and explained to him my desires. Bill humored me, regarded me for a moment and then recommended I get a little older before trying anything so ambitious. I was disappointed. The following week after church, he waved Dad and I over and gave me a signed copy of his book *Nature I Loved* and a letter. He said he had arranged for me to go to a Conservation School (like a summer camp) held each summer for a few weeks. He wanted to sponsor me, if it was alright with my folks. It was, although I think it was difficult for my mom who, originally an old-timey Baptist, had a thing about accepting charity of any kind. I remember some...friction.

My parents couldn't have afforded any sort of summer camp for me, so the Conservation School was a great opportunity. There would be orienteering, gun safety, shooting, canoeing...that sort of stuff.

I read the book Bill gave me, and it only served to get my juices going even more. If you haven't read *Nature I Loved* I still recommend it, sixty years after its publication. Basically, it's about Bill going through the typical "I don't know what to do with myself and it's freaking the folks out" phase of life, when he buys a rundown camp on Hermon Pond, not far from Bangor. His plan was to go there, fix it up and live in it for at least a year on his own and with little or no help from anyone. He did, and the story of his time on the lake (it's technically a lake) is a great one.

His experiences were filled with a few disasters, more than a few poignant moments and some witty methods of making money in the middle of nowhere. (Hermon Pond was a lot more remote then and there were only a few cottages on the lake. There are probably subdivisions now.) There was also quite a bit of fly fishing in the book and I think from those pages came the first real interest for me in casting a fly.

Mr. Geagan went on from his time in that cabin to become a newspaper man, an illustrator and a conservationist. And I went on to Conservation School at Branch Pond to learn outdoor stuff. Yes, it was a great experience, I suppose. I could have gotten so much more out of it, but it was my first time away from home. I was so nervous, I wet the bed the first night. I had had a three year dry spell and felt relatively sure I was out of the woods. I was raised a devout Catholic, so I was sure this was a punishment right from God. Probably for having so many impure thoughts about girls—a recently acquired skill and maybe the only thing I was good at. Anyhow, I was discovered, and was so rattled from the event that I never fully recovered mentally until I got home.

Of course, I participated in all the classes, and during letter writing time, I wrote a long, thankful letter to Mr. Geagan. I told him how great the school was and all the things that happened from day to day, leaving out the nighttime problem, of course. I was even worse at writing then than I am now, and when he read it he most likely realized I was "special" (we didn't call it A.D.D. then, we were just "slow"). I do remember thinking when the week was over that my own father knew a lot more about animal behavior, tracking, surviving in the wild, shooting, swimming, and just about everything else than the instructors there. I always looked up to him (most everyone did), but after that realization, I respected him even more. For years, instead of him going out of his way to try and teach me outdoor things, I *asked* him more often.

In the 1970's there used to be the Surplus Store in downtown Bangor on Main Street. I saved up lawn-mowing money the summer after the Branch Pond calamity and bought an entire fly fishing outfit for about eighteen dollars. It was fiberglass, the reel was attached, and not only was the line on the reel, but so was the leader, a fly (a Royal Coachman) and, get this, it was strung up! All I had to do was stick the ferrules together and start casting. I remember the butt of the rod just above the cork grip was, like, an inch in diameter and although it said it was a seven weight rod, it was really more like a twelve. It was perfect for fishing small brooks in Maine...or for tuna. Anyway, it's what I could afford. It was some years before I sat on it and broke it. I seem to sit on fly rods a lot. It's a thing.

I eventually grew up, somewhat, and my fly fishing became more refined over the years. When I was single, I became one of those guys who would eat nothing but Ramen Noodles for five weeks so I could buy a three-hundred dollar reel. I was still in the "elementary school" phase of angling when one of my six sisters finally married a fly fisherman...a serious fly fisher.

It was Chuck Green of Winterport who taught me the most about the art of the cast, all the knots I needed to know and about the insect world that fly fishing revolves within. Chuck is a world-class fly caster and I believe he's a member of the Federation of Fly Casters or some such thing. I'm not much of a joiner, so I'm not sure. He was a casting instructor for Orvis for some time. I've seen some pretty famous fly fishers cast (ones you've heard of) and Chuck is the best I've ever seen. Now he's the Director of Fly Fishing at Hidden Meadows Ranch in Arizona.

On the Roach River, many years ago, Chuck decided it was time he taught me how to nymph properly. I watched him catch five or six good size salmon before I finally hooked one. He has been known to pull his truck up to a well-known pool on a famous river, wade into it with cut off shorts and a grungy old fly vest, and catch big fish out from under the noses of some pretty frustrated, well-dressed anglers. Then he'd climb back into his truck and drive off—all in just a few minutes. Chuck has a biology degree.

In his prime (*our* prime), Chuck would fish in any weather, anytime of day or night and never complain. He was always up for just about any fishing excursion and used to tie pretty acceptable flies.

61

Here's the most important thing in my mind about Chuck's fishing; he would fish for any species of fish there is and they were all interesting to him. Sure, he'd probably rather catch an Atlantic Salmon than, say, a perch, but if perch was what was around, he'd have fun fishing for them.

I think Chuck instilled that same open-minded approach to fly fishing in me along the way, and *that* is what has kept me interested in fly fishing in such a fashion...that is to say, passionate. I have felt the same way about fishing for various species for decades. Perhaps if I only wanted to fish for salmon and trout, like many folks, I might have lost a little enthusiasm from time to time. I've always been interested in far too many things in this life (it drives my wife nuts) and I'm easily distracted, even at my age, but the fly fishing is always the acme of fervidness. In part, Chuck Green is to blame for that.

Chuck and I have lost touch for the most part, he lives in the Southwest, and I'm back in Maine. We communicate every year or two, partly because I am still rebelling against the Facebook thing believing it is just one more avenue that leads to even more unnecessary conversations in a world of many. I'm told I'm being ridiculous about that and overthinking the whole mass-media, communication cyber community. I probably am...but I do send occasional emails and I still know how to pick up a telephone.

So yeah, I'd have to say Chuck Green has been an important part of my life, because when life's considerations smack me right between the eyes, I've always had fly fishing to relax me and help regain my balance and my vision, and without his influence, I might not have always had that counsel.

My son is sixteen now. It has been great fun teaching him the same things Dad, Chuck and Bill taught me and to watch him grow into an amazing fly fisher. Half the time when we fish, I end up sitting on a rock upstream from him and I just watch him cast, in perfect rhythm, nothing hurried, and with great patience for a young man, finding within himself a pure and secular peace. On a couple of those occasions, I've caught myself looking at the whole scene before me, but from somewhere else...and suddenly I realize that *I'm* Dad, and the boy is me. It quickly gets to be too much for me, and I turn and make a cast, across and a little upstream, with a small mend in the line, the way Chuck taught me.

That boy, who's really a young man now, will be going off to college in a year-and-a half, and we'll fish together less. But I truly find solace in the fact that no matter what happens to me in the future, he will always have fly fishing to help him find *his* vision. Last year, my twelve-year-old daughter learned to cast. Late in the season, for the first time, I watched her spot a rise, pay out some line, make a perfect cast with my three-weight and hook, play and carefully release a small bass. It was something to see.

And yes, we occasionally do fish for bass these days—on purpose sometimes—thanks to Chuck. And if my father saw from Heaven my girl catch that fish last summer, I'm sure he was smiling, and I bet he could care less that it wasn't a brook trout. Everybody wins...even the bass, who didn't get wacked in the end.

Southern Fishing

Pleasant River Lake 2007

Mountains were a big part of my life for a long time. I got the climbing bug before moving to Jackson Hole, Wyoming as a young man, but it was there it came to a head. Living, growing and mucking around in the mountains near Jackson, for years it was as if I was in the right place, at the right time, meeting just the right people to get me into tight spots every day. It wasn't long before I ended up in Lima, Peru, looking to climb bigger mountains. Fortunate to climb in many parts of the world, I always seemed to return to the Andes. There were other things as important to me then as the climbing...culture, remoteness, caves, adventure and fly fishing. Lima was a pretty good jumping-off spot for other mountains and volcanoes in South America, and for a young, energetic man, life was good.

Living for years at a time out of a 5,800 cubic inch Lowe backpack can eventually become a Zen art form. You have to have this, can live without that...but the one thing I could never live without was my four-piece 5-weight Sage fly rod. I seldom went anywhere without it. I also carried the least expensive LL Bean reel (which I purchased to replace the old Pflueger a cow stepped on in Idaho) with the cheapest weight-forward floating line I could find, and an extra spool with a fast sink-tip line. There was a single fly box which served as my entire tackle box...it took the place of my fly vest, fly boxes, everything rolled into a 1"x4"x7" container.

In it I carried (from what I can remember); a tiny homemade vise made from a couple of old recycled surgical instruments, a couple of tapered leaders, two spools of tippit material (4# 3x and 2# 5x), a few pieces of split shot, some nail clippers, and only two or three rows of flies near the top of the box. That was all the room there was left for flies. I remember very well what I would carry for flies. There were four or five wooly buggers, mostly black with a couple of olive, about six elk-hair caddis flies (big ones), some size 8 streamers; two muddler minnows, two grey ghosts, two Mickey Finns, six or eight nymphs, a couple of hare's ears, some pheasant tails, and a few big black stone flies. I did have a couple of other fly-tying tools with me then, but never any materials.

I was a bona fide new–age, funked-out, live-by-your-wits, gorp-eating wannabe - adventurer in those days. I subscribed to the cool idea that if I could catch fish in foreign countries with flies that I tied myself, well, how great was that? If I tied the flies with scrounged, non-fly-tying stuff, well, then that's even cooler. And scrounge I did! I remember snipping hair from friends dogs, cats and, with permission, children. Once I talked a flight attendant from Faucett Airlines into giving me enough of her own hair to make a half-dozen of the loveliest black whooly buggers you ever did see (they were weighted, with little red heads and no hackle). I did have a bobbin, but I would pilfer thread from wherever I was billeting at the time. Head cement? Try Superglue. I'm sure this all sounds like blasphemy to some of you purists, but remember two things: one; I'm a crappy fly-tier on a good day, with real equipment, and two; in those years I sometimes had to decide whether I was going to take along an extra piece of climbing gear, or underwear. Remember the slogan "Climb Commando!"? Well, that probably wasn't a slogan...but it could've been. Anyway, being innovative with fly-tying seemed if not romantic, necessary.

Although I never was able to fish for the big browns or rainbows in Argentina, I was fortunate enough to fish the Urubamba, Amazon, Canete, and Orinoca Rivers, lots of mountain lakes and many small brooks and streams—some of which I never learned the names of. I had my favorites. After I got the obligatory piranha under my belt (any fly will work, providing you rub them with some leftover steak and beat the water with the rod tip) and peacock bass, I could settle down and try to catch some trout. In the years since, when I think of fishing down south, a couple of places always dominate the ever-expanding crevices of my mind.

Peru is a magical place, with a remarkably varied topography, friendly people and great music. I loved it for lots of reasons, but one of the best things about it, aside from the people, was the fact that I could be in Cuzco on Monday, shoot over to the Manus and sweat in the jungle by Wednesday, be in Huaraz by Friday and, weather permitting, be sun bathing on a glacier by Sunday...albeit with altitude sickness. Most importantly, with careful economy of time, I could fish in each place.

Huaraz, about 150 miles north of Lima, is my favorite Peruvian town. I've been around the world three times and Huaraz is one of the few places I actually thought of ditching everything (which often wasn't much) and becoming an ex-patriot...for good (another was Portobelo Panama). I met a lot of ex-pats along the way, and it's definitely doable. I used to think, maybe I could write a book about it, like Scott Nearing, only it would be "Living the Irresponsible Life."

It would become famous...a kind of operating manual for folks who don't want to deal with life's considerations—complete with instructions on just how long one can go without bathing before getting cooties, or how to recognize federales at the bar (I actually got good at that).

Huaraz is a town of, at the time, about 100,000 citizens. It's about an eight-hour bus ride (depending upon the bus) north of Lima. The ride, like a lot of bus rides in South America, can be harrowing. The first time I took the ride north from Lima, along the winding, narrow highway towards Huaraz, the steep, sandy cliffs falling straight down into the sea, the old bus clearly the victim of faulty steering linkage, reminded me of my father's old International pickup. My Dad would barrel down the Airline in Washington County, Maine. Working hard to keep the truck between the birches, he would turn the steering wheel a full half-turn before the front wheels would respond. He always said he could "feel the road beneath him." (I would say some smart-ass thing like, "...am I going to be feeling it with my face?") The bus was kind of like that...only, I trusted my Dad. But could I trust this Peruvian, who seemed like he would rather be just about anywhere else? Guess so, because in all those years I never expired in a flaming bus, and I was *so* sure that I would.

While Lima sits in a coastal desert, Huaraz is snuggled into hilly upland country, looking straight up into the Cordillera Blanca...the white mountains of the Andes. The unofficial trekking and climbing capital of South America, Huaraz has it all...museums, lively night life (and I mean *lively*), archaeology, restaurants, lots of artisans, natural hot springs, and as I said, very friendly folks. The atmosphere is much more laid-back than most tourist spots in Peru—or anywhere in South America for that matter. When I was there it was also less expensive. Whether a visitor, tourist, a trekker, or a climber, you could expect to find people who were helpful without being pushy. We made scores of trips into the Cordillera, climbing every mountain we could.

The most popular trek in the area is undoubtedly the Huayhuash circuit trek. I believe it's one of the best treks in the world. A hiker can work out many variations of routes through the Cordillera, and almost all will eventually take you along some of the most beautiful mountain streams and glacial lakes anywhere. Although I was definitely into my share of peak bagging in those days, it was alongside those streams that I have some of my choicest memories. While climbing clients were cooling their feet in the cold water, I was quickly flailing the water with the floating line, long leaders and some kind of a scud or hare's ear nymph. In the late 1800's, someone stocked many of the lakes with rainbow trout and they're still there. Some of them, in certain lakes, are very, very big (like...twelve-plus pounds big). Most lakes hold fish in the eight to sixteen inch range. The streams, in my experience, seem to average around nine-inch fish.

The climbing in the Cordillera was epic...Pisco, Huascaran, Yerupaja, Siula Grande...the list goes on and on—stunning peaks, shining white glaciers against what seems like perpetual indigo blue skies. (They might not have been indigo, but I was almost always looking at the peaks through a polarizing filter on my Nikon.) The streams ran through wonderful high mountain meadows, knee-high grasses interrupted constantly by big stands of eight-foot diameter clumps of pastel blue lupines. Unlike here in Maine, the lupines in Peru bloom for a couple of months. At about ten thousand feet above sea level, scattered along the edges of the valley floors, are the craziest plants; called Puya raimondii, these things are enormous. From the lower bushy base of the plant shoots a large spike of rosettes, growing over twenty feet tall. Also called Queen of the Andes, they have more than 3,000 flowers and millions of seeds. It's a bromeliad, so parts of it looks a little pineapple-esque and it can take forty to 100 years to flower. Once it does, it dies...kind of like mayflies. They're only found in a few places in the Andes. It must be spectacular to see them in bloom, especially with the backdrop of one of the glaciers of the Cordillera

Blanca. I was never that lucky. I saw clients sit and stare at them up close for twenty minutes, as if they were trying to wrap their heads around them.

I remember fishing Soltera Cocha lake for the first time. I sat under a great old quenual tree, which resembles a cross between a mesquite and an apple tree (without the apples), tying on a small muddler minnow with a bead head pheasant tail dropper. I was accustomed to never seeing any top water action. The surfaces of the crystal blue lakes have never been violated by a mayfly, which is just too bad. I was missing the mayflies when old friend Thor Kiezer (a world–class climber and all around good guy) plunked down beside me. I had put about two hours between myself and the rest of the party in an effort to buy some time to fish, so I was surprised to see him. He said, "Shitty view isn't it?" We gazed up the valley from our spot beneath the tree, not a road, building or person in sight, past the perfect blue lakes, the pastel colors of the wildflowers, the whiter than white glaciers against the darker blue sky capped with wisps of lenticular clouds. "Yeah," I replied. "They should fix this up a little."

After Thor had a couple of snorts from his water bottle, he mentioned the glaciers. The year was 1986 and, although I had been in the area many times over the previous few years, he had been guiding climbing trips in the Cordillera for over ten years. "You see that arroyo running down the left side of the valley?" he asked. I nodded. "And the grey rock band between the lake and the glacier?" "Yep," I said, and looked back at Thor. "That rock band was all glacier eight years ago," he said. I snapped my head back towards the glacier. He was telling me that the glacier had receded a good hundred and fifty feet back up the mountain, in eight years...not very scientific or accurate, but impressive just the same. Nobody in my circles had been talking about global warming in those days. It wasn't for another few years that I heard about "holes in the ozone." I regarded carefully the glaciers I was on or near, around the world, after that. I was an archaeology student for some years, and was aware of many climate changes throughout the ages. I remember reading that the average temperatures in Europe in the Middle Ages were significantly warmer than those in modern times. I don't know much about climate change, but Thor's comment was eye-opening for me that day...I doubt he ever knew that.

After talking a while longer, we were interrupted when my big backpack went floating by on the back of one of our burros. He (the burro) stopped when he caught site of us. One of the arrieros (burro wrangler) came scooting along the trail next, and with no apparent thought, gave the burro (carrying *my* pack, which always made me feel a little guilty) a swift kick in the ass. (Quite literally, come to think of it.) My burro's head jerked up and he took off down the trail again, the arriero giving us a smile and a wave as he went by. Thor said, "Man! If I ever get reincarnated, I hope I don't come back as a burro in Peru." "Well...if you do," I replied, "I hope I come back as an arriero." He laughed, shouldered his pack, glanced at my fly rod and left, yelling back, "Bring me three or four!" He should've known by then I seldom kept the fish I caught. I started down to the edge of the lake.

The lakes are spectacular in part because of the intense aqua blue. Silty glacial run-off lessens the visibility in the water. My journal reads that I figured the visibility was about four feet near the surface, but I knew so little about anything at that age, I'm sure I was wrong. I never saw much vegetation in any of the alpine lakes more than three or four feet from water's edge. I could, though, appreciate ledges and drop-offs. The big problem on my early tries was what flies to use. As I mentioned, the selection was small, but I did have a vise. Years before, I had spent some effort trying to figure out the correct approach.

Here's what I learned fishing those lakes. The first few attempts were youthful, charge-ahead casting practice sessions, all alone in those beautiful mountain cirques, tossing fly after fly until I finally hooked something. It's not that it wasn't great fun...it was, but it was also mindless. The third or fourth time in the Cordillera I took the time to stop and think it over. I remember plunking down on a rock overlooking the two Llanganuco Lakes. And thinking, "What is it I *do* know about these lakes?" Well, I did know these lakes were always cold, so the trout wouldn't need to travel to a comfort zone. These lakes were not stratified...meaning they probably didn't "turn over" in the spring after ice-out. There were almost no tree-lined shores, so I wouldn't be limited to roll casts. Whereas Rainbows must spawn in moving water, from an angler's point of view, the inlets and outlets were worth some effort. Also, if I was to fish aquatic insect patterns, I would remember that still-water insects do much more swimming than those in swift-moving water. There didn't seem to be any leaches present. There were the odd beetles and spiders in the low bushes that dotted the shores. Not much info, but a start.

So I stuck to streamers and nymphs. Eventually I picked up a few nice fish with the grey ghosts, and even a couple on the muddler minnows. But this day, on the shore of Soltera Cocha, things were going to be different. I had a deadly weapon..."Ole killer."

Back in Lima a couple of weeks earlier, I had found an athletic store in Miraflores and amongst the mountains of soccer equipment, I found some fish hooks. About size eight, they were probably designed for live bait...they had a strange bend built into the shank, but I could straighten them out. There were also some packages of thin strips of lead which the locals use as sinkers while eel fishing in the surf near Lima. The strips were quite malleable and I hoped to build them into some flies for the upcoming trip to the Cordillera. A few weeks earlier we had run a trip to Machu Picchu from the Incan city Ollantaytambo by way of the Inca Trail. Along the way I had collected some feathers I found here and there. There were some brown, green and red ones, and two blue feathers that looked surprisingly like they were from a Blue Jay. The collection, in a zip-lock baggie, was kept in the same pocket of my pack as the "tackle box." These feathers, along with the lead strips and a little tinsel (all of the friends I made in Peru were Catholics, so a little Christmas tinsel wasn't hard to find), would have to do for some streamer flies for the alpine lakes high in the Andes. I doubted they would work, but the collecting, tying and the innovating was half the fun.

I tied the flies in the hotel my first night in Huaraz, spreading the feathers over the little end table in my room. The feathers reminded me of the little sparrow-like birds I knew I would see in a few days at about 13,000 feet above sea level. Most trips up high in that region it would get pretty cold at night. In the mornings, as soon as the sunlight would wind its way between the mountains and hit us with that wonderful, warm glow, the arrieros would walk around camp, checking the low bushes for the birds. If they were caught out in the open in the previous evening, they would spend the night, freezing, clinging to the branches. They would get so cold, their heart rate seemed to slow and they were too cold to fly. The arrieros would poke around, in a rather workman-like manner, gathering up the birds they could find. They would cradle them in their hands, blow on them, and sometimes even tuck the birds gently in their shirts. As soon as the birds would start to flutter, the boys would hold them in their flattened-out palms and, when ready, they would fly off. It's pretty cool—beautiful, actually. Quickly, we all did it and it became quite the ritual. And no...I never did harvest any fly-tying materials "on the wing." Anyway, there was no bird flu that we knew of in those days.

I slid the hooks and lead strips to the left, clamped the vice to the table—with a piece of cardboard under the clamp—and the feathers to the right. I snipped a couple of strands of the blue-green, yarn-like material that made the fringes along the edges of the bedspread. (You really couldn't tell.) A tiny bead of super glue along the shank of the hook held the twisted piece of lead in place. I found that I needed to wait a few moments to let the glue get tacky first. Then the aforementioned tinsel was wrapped over the lead and tied at both ends with red thread for the body. I pulled apart one of the bluish pieces of yarn so it became very sparse and resembled dubbing. I tied it below the head so it ran under the shank and trimmed it so it barely covered the bend in the hook. Then I used some wisps of a red feather for the throat. I simply picked a couple of the best looking feathers for the wings...ones that seemed to lay down the best. It was finished with a red head. It looked like crap. It was messy...head cement would have been *so* much better! There are a lot of great fly tyers in Maine. None of their flies had thread and bubbles of hardened super glue hanging off of them. But possibly, just possibly- it would be the best looking streamer the trout in Soltera Colcha have ever seen. They might even eat it. I tied a few more before running out of suitable material.

Before tying on "Ole Killer," I found a nice spot near the head of the lake. I could stand on some prominent rock slabs where I could see two underwater ledges spreading out away from me, like the sides of a funnel, in increasing depths. A simple thirty-foot cast, in virtually no wind, I dropped Killer just inside the seam of the right-hand side of the funnel. It sank fast with the sink tip line and the weighted hook. I had used a shorter leader hoping to keep the hook down. After waiting twenty seconds, a quick retrieve, five inches at a time—nothing. A second cast yielded the same result. The third cast was a bit further from the ledge, in deeper water.

Then, bang! Half-way through the retrieve, there was a fish on, in that aqua-blue, sterile looking water. It wasn't a heavy fish, but it fought well. I striped it in, in a rather business-like manner. (I really wanted a good look at it in case I couldn't hook another.) It was a rainbow alright. Not a lot of color, but a trout, about twelve-inches long and slender.

I have no problem killing trout and salmon nowadays, in certain waters and in certain situations, but in those days I was strictly catch-and-release. So off she swam, back out of sight into that pristine alpine lake. After growing up fishing the brooks and rivers of Maine, and years of fishing for trout in Wyoming, Montana and Idaho, I remember thinking as I watched her swim away, about her existence in this lake. This fish, a descendant of a stocking program and never experiencing a caddis hatch, or tasting a green drake, or what must seem like an injection of protein when consuming a leach (or maybe it's more like decadence...like a double hot fudge sundae), lives here in South America, never bumping into any other fish except for other silvery rainbows. Did she feel, well...incarcerated? Is that why she came to the shore grudgingly, instead of belligerently? Is that why she never jumped? I don't know, but I do know that I caught a bunch more fish on that fly, and released 'em all. My journal at the time suggests at least twenty, and that's what I remember...but I've never been much of a head counter.

We all have our own relationships with nature, whether it's in our hearts or in our souls, and a smarter man in that place, at that time might have grown a little. I don't remember feeling any existential tingly feeling or anything...but I do remember realizing how damned lucky I was.

A couple of hours before it became dark (dark comes quick, that high in the mountains), I packed up and struck off around the lake to the campsite. As I strode into camp with the rod tube strapped to my day pack, fishless and tired as heck, I caught Thor's eye. "Well! It's the great white fisherman! Did you bring me any?" "Nah," I shook my head. "There's no fish in that ditch."

Fairy Tales

Blue Hill, June 2010

When I was maybe nine or ten years old I remember going with Dad over to "The Goode's" camp, which was around the cove from our own place on Pleasant River Lake in the township of Beddington. Lennie Goode seemed to run the camp, more or less, but at that time the older Grandpa was still there, sitting on the porch, in his green Dickie work pants which were held up by black braces, in his white t-shirt, casting over all he surveyed through horn-rimmed glasses. He must have been in his seventies at that time.

It was Lennie who did most of the talking, as I remember, and although I can't recall one thing Lennie told me (I was pretty young), I do remember the only conversation I ever had with Grandpa. (I'll call him Grandpa...I'm not sure what his family called him.)

He told me two things. He liked and often ate chubs, and that Canoe Brook, which was nothing more than a trickle where it flowed into the west side of the lake not far from our camp, had some deadwater upstream that he fished when he was a young man (the 1930's) where he had caught some very big brookies. He kept referring to them in pounds, not inches. Years later he saw some eighteen inch trout from there, caught by other fishermen, but said he didn't think it had been fished for a very long time—emphasis on very. The seed was planted.

There were no roads to the west side of Pleasant River Lake in those days, so to fish Canoe Brook you had to take a boat along the lakeshore to the inlet and then hike upstream, hopping from boulder to boulder, and through some blow-downs to get to the deadwater.

Back at camp, I excitedly mentioned the notion of making the trip as soon as possible with Dad, and it became obvious that it was not something my mother was too keen on. The furtive glances my Mom shot at Dad weren't as furtive as she thought. A can of worms had been opened. Apparently Dad-ee-O heard the same fish stories years before and had gone there alone, when I was just a toddler. (I don't remember being a toddler, but at some point, I'm told, I toddled.) Dad's version was lovely and appropriately adventurous. A tale of hiking up the tiny trickle, through the beautiful cedars, hopping from boulder-to-boulder and finally the dark forest opened up to a pristine stretch of dark, deep, hardly flowing deadwater. The water was deep enough to stay cool in the summer, with nice undercut banks on both sides to hide trout. He told how he hooked two trout in his first two casts at the tail of the deadwater. When he tried to work his way farther upstream to the best looking water he got stuck in the mud, and sank up to his arm pits, and got so tired struggling free from the grip of the wet humus that he eventually went back to camp. Oh...and he said there probably are nice trout in there. At last he said, as if it was one of life's missed opportunities, "I always wanted to go back and drag a canoe in there."

Mom's version was a little different. Hers was more about how he got stuck so badly it took him three hours to get unstuck; she spoke of how he lost the two trout he had in his creel and he arrived back at camp after dark with only one shoe. Oh, and of course she mentioned, nobody knew exactly where he was and how she might have been left alone with eight children...the favorite just a toddler. She never mentioned the pretty cedars, and she never let Dad go back there. I threatened to go from time to time as I got older, but never made it.

As I stumbled my way through adulthood (and I do mean *stumbled*), I returned to Maine as often as possible. When I did, I would always make the pilgrimage down to camp. (In Maine the correct verbiage is "upta camp" but we always said "downta camp." I don't know why.) I would fish the Pleasant River, Mopang Stream and lots of other nearby brooks. I would always give Canoe Brook and its monster trout a lot of consideration. I'm referring to them as monster trout here because as my adolescent brain remembered the old stories, the fish got bigger and bigger (Why break with tradition?). Eventually Canoe Brook took on legendary status...at least to me. Since the relatively abundant six to eight pound native brook trout, once available in Maine, went the way of the Dodo a long time ago, the thought of at least four or five-pound fish hidden away in a little bogan near our camp evolved into what seemed like plausible wishful thinking.

A couple of weeks ago I was down to camp for a work weekend with my family. The ride in on the dirt road is different than in the old days...you can drive right in to camp now. There's no more carrying all of the dunnage around the cove on an uneven path through the woods from where we parked. There now is a road along the entire west side of the lake, with access roads jutting down to the shore where new camps will be springing up soon. Times change.

A mile or so from camp the new road crosses Canoe Brook a couple of thousand feet from the lakeshore. The tiny brook runs through a culvert which has created a little plunge pool below it. For the last few years, it seems like every time we drove over the culvert, I glanced upstream and wondered. The cedars, mossy banks and the little pocket-water looked so appealing. I paused there on the culvert once or twice, to tell an abbreviated version of the old story to my young family. "Yes kids," I'd say, "nearly sixty years ago, your grandfather walked right through here...of course the culvert wasn't here then, or the road..." but to them it was less a story than another old anecdote, which is natural. A couple of times when down to camp alone, I stopped on the way out and caught a few tiny brookies in the pool below the culvert on an elk-hair caddis. I was always too busy to make the trip up to the deadwater, even though I reckoned by the Delorme, the fishable water was only about an eighth of a mile from the new road.

On the first evening of this last trip to camp, I was pouring over some old topo maps which were almost ripped to shreds now from overuse and announced, "Son, tomorrow we're hiking up Canoe Brook." It was as if there was nothing I could do about it. "Cool," was all he said. Obviously, he didn't hear Grandpa Goode tell the story.

I have fly fished all over the world, and have spent a couple of summers in the town of Allagash fishing the back-water bogans along the Little Black River (I mention the bogans because a dim-witted angler can get stuck in the mud there also, trust me.). Looking at the maps, I had no doubt that our new-fangled breathable waders, $100 wading staffs and our expensive fly rods would be sufficient to negotiate the deadwater. We were off to conquer the story itself.

Any hatches near the end of May wouldn't come off until late morning, so we got on the water around 7:30 a.m. and struck off straight up the stream bed. It was indeed beautiful, but a little worrisome that the deepest water we came across was only about twelve to eighteen inches deep.

After less than thirty minutes of a good, hard pace we were there. The sky *did* open up and exposed a large marshy bogan. Sure enough, there was a section of deadwater flowing through it...typical of so many Washington County brooks and streams. About fifty feet wide in most places and seemingly quite deep, the brook flowed through an open, grassy expanse, dotted with the skeletons of long-dead spruce and fir trees. Indian pitcher plants were scattered everywhere. We found it interesting that what held the water back was a line of boulders and gravel which stretched across the stream almost as if someone placed them there. But of course, it was a glacier that dropped them there, deposited in its wake like huge droppings.

It was very windy that particular morning, so casting was a little difficult. There was no hatch coming off, my heartburn was acting up and my reel seat was a little loose...aw Hell, we were just skunked! It's probably worth noting that as we first started to fish, I walked gingerly up to the water's edge and tried stepping onto a partially exposed tree root. I put a small amount of weight onto it (which is particularly hard for me to do) and started sinking immediately. I stepped back to make some casts from the tall marsh grass. On my first cast, I heard a grunt coming from my son, about fifty feet upstream. One step and he was in up past his groin, struggling to get out. I yelled to check with him and he waved me off. I watched him pull and push and eventually work himself free. He was out when I got to him. It was a good thing he had boot-foot waders. He was a tall fifteen-year-old then and didn't have an ounce of fat on him, but he was pretty tired.

As I looked at the boy, his waders covered in mud, I remembered some of the details Mom mentioned about Dad's adventure, like, "being alone so far up there, there was no sense in your father bothering to yell for help," and "it took him more than three hours to work himself free." His shirt had mud in the breast pockets. Turns out, Mom's version was probably pretty accurate.

We tried caddis flies, mayflies and nymphs with no luck. We forgot to bring the woolly buggers we had just tied. Things were said like, "I'd like to be here in the evening, when there's a hatch," and "Yeah, I bet this brook would come alive!"

The wind got worse and we decided to head to a different stream nearby where we would be fishing in a more protected area. As we headed back to the Jeep I said, rather matter-of-factly, and without thinking, "We've got to come back and drag a canoe up there."

Underdogs

Allagash, Maine 1998

Americans love underdogs, when we recognize them. There are underdog fish out there, and while some are prized game fish, some, are not so loved. There are game fish, trash fish, pan fish, blue fish (with apologies, Dr. Seuss). I happen to like all of the lesser known, less fished-for trout. Out west I guess they would be the Golden, the Apache, the Greenback, the Bull, and the Yellowstone Cutthroat. There are probably a bunch more, but as I said...they're lesser known.

Here in Maine, it has got to be the Blueback trout (*Salvelinus oquassa*), sometimes mistakenly called the Sunapee trout (*S. aureolus*). Ever since I can remember I've had a soft spot in my heart for the Bluebacks.

One of my favorite books as a child was the 1912 Sir Arthur Conan Doyle classic novel Lost World. For a kid who longed for adventure, it was super cool. In the book, in a vast, remote region, large tracts of land had been thrust skyward by some geophysical activity in ancient times, as if one day God shoved His (or Her) hand up from underneath the ground and said, "Okay...now, this piece we're going to separate from the rest so that nobody can screw it up." Huge plateaus were isolated from all surrounding areas, and life on top had remained untouched by the evolutionary processes below for millennia. Doyle had Neanderthals running around with the likes of Cro-Magnons. There were even dinosaurs. Awesome! It was a mess that was made worse by throwing twentieth century Europeans into the mix. (As so often was the case.) Sound crazy? *Maybe.*

I knew when I first read the book I would someday travel to that place, and I did in my late twenties. Mt. Roraima and The Lost World is in southern Venezuela, in La Gran Sabana. Called Tepuis (the local Pemon Indian name for mountain), the tallest of those mountains is Roraima, and reports of its first ascent were the inspiration for The Lost World. It is very remote, near the Brazilian border and is a paradise for outdoor types. It has vast plains, about a dozen micro-climates, mountains, rivers, and waterfalls that dominate the landscape. I did find the Tepuis, but no dinosaurs—nor prehistoric men. But I did find one wacked-out Belgian on acid.

I'll digress a little. In one of the remotest parts of the world I've ever seen were an incredible number of social drop-outs, ex-pats and folks on the lam.

They're not bothered by anybody and they seem to live in their own little artist communities. You can find interesting people like that all over the planet, but in La Gran Sabana (The Great Plain) it seemed to be, I don't know, the next level I guess. I spent a couple of weeks exploring caves trying to photograph Narison bats, climbed a couple of Tepuis and fished a few streams that had *jasper* stream beds. I met a group of artists living in a homemade house completely off the grid, making tie-died t-shirts and shipping them internationally. The same bush pilot I hired to fly me there from Caracas, picked up a shipment of the shirts every other month, landing on a gravel runway the artisans had built themselves. His name was Manuel and, although he was a solid guy through-and-through, he didn't have a working starter in his old Cessna. I had to grab the prop and give it a spin and dive out of the way each time we wanted to go anywhere. I eventually got comfortable with it, and as it turned out, it was a skill I would employ in equally remote locations later in life. I stayed with "the guys" as I called them (although they were mostly women) in that little utopia for a few days before they invited me to stay. It was tempting...they had a hot tub, a jury-rigged still that produced some pretty good hootch, and a winery, of sorts.

But Doyle's isolation theory does hold water, at least at a rudimentary level. There *are* plants and even insects living on top of some of the Tepuis that don't exist anywhere else. They've been unmolested for thousands of years...till now. A lot of tourists travel to the Sabana just to see Angel Falls and then go home. For me Angel Falls might have been the least interesting thing there. If you're going to go all that distance and at such an expense, you might as well bum around and get into some trouble. Make it worthwhile.

Is that digressing enough for a story about fishing for Blueback trout in Maine? The point is the power of isolation.

Around 10,000 years ago in present day Maine, chunks of ice from the last ice age started melting, leaving in its path moraines, rivers, lakes, boulders and future blueberry fields. One fish theory is that a few species of anadromous fish became landlocked. Fish like Atlantic salmon and Arctic charr. I've even talked to some people who believe the landlocked salmon we know and love today were sea-run Atlantic salmon that (250 years ago) had become physically landlocked by man-made dams (those pesky Europeans again). Most biologists believe the landlocking was a gradual "voluntary" process...and I mean gradual. The sea-run fish did not get to Green

Lake and think, "now, this is the life! I am *not* leaving!"

The general consensus from the biologists I've talked to don't believe the "stranded by the glaciers" theory. Most fisheries professionals just subscribe to varying stages of adaptation. It gets complicated. The Glacier Theory is usually bantered about by non-scientific locals. It is romantic, but really, during the ice age, Maine was covered by sheets of ice thousands of feet thick. What could survive that? Wait a tick! Maybe that's how all those Irish folks ended up in the Allagash...*they're* tough enough. A little ice never stopped them. (One spring in the 1990's an enormous ice jam caused severe flooding in the towns of Dicky and Allagash, and folks were stranded in homes and in a church along the St. John River. The stormy, nighttime weather grounded the National Guard, the State Police, the Sheriff's Department, and everyone else. Tyler Kelly, a local fishing and hunting guide of some renown, had to boat them all out by flashlight and feel. Ice floes the size of houses took out trees and roads, but Kelly got 'em all out...in a canoe.

So...following deglaciation, Arctic charr were some of the first fish to populate fresh water in present day New England. Today, most serious anglers from New England who fish for a wide variety of fish species, I call us "cross-fishers," know there are still some of these charr around. As a youngster I had heard about

Bluebacks a few times, but got much more interested in them as I got older and started fly fishing. One of the best ways to learn things is to ask a lot of questions, which I did. I asked other flyfishers, bait fishermen, old-timers, sporting goods people, friends and family. It became apparent that hardly anyone knew much at all about them, so I called the Maine Department of Fish and Wildlife and *that* is how I found Fred Kircheis. He's long retired now, but when I first met him he was a fisheries research biologist with the DIFW and a world's leading authority regarding Blueback trout. He also happens to be a gracious man, eager to teach if you ask the questions.

I remember his old office in Bangor. It was a miracle of fishy information—especially about charr. Among the books on the shelves, were jars of formalin containing tiny rare fish—at the time recently discovered. Here and there were old artifacts of Maine's logging days, back when men were tough as nails. Every flat surface held pamphlets, books and articles about Arctic charr. There, in that office, was every bit of known information about Blueback trout. I was in the right place.

To understand the difference between Bluebacks and their cousins, the Sunapee trout, we would have to talk about things like mitochondria and restriction enzymes. I'm not going to do that...mostly because I'm numb as a hake when it comes to real science.

Let's just say that there are subtle differences, each with different geographical histories. The fact is, not much is known about the life history and the ecology of the Bluebacks...at least not in the early 1990's when I was learning about them. Although effective management of fish populations depends upon a full understanding of the species, along with cooperation from the public, these beautiful fish might not be doomed. The good news is that as they have evolved, the Bluebacks require deep, cold and remote lakes. Difficult access should help them survive. At one time, the research staff in Bangor consisted of five field research biologists. When I met with Mr. Kircheis he was the only one. He told me that Bluebacks had never been raised in a hatchery and they had never documented the spawn. He said, "We know they spawn in the fall, and that's about it."

He knew the Bluebacks were very similar to lake trout in their habits.

The more I learned about these fish, the more I regarded them as a sort of underdog. One friend of mine remembers his uncle telling him stories of Bluebacks in Maine's most northern county, "so thick they parted the water as we waded in to swim" and people netting them by the hundreds to use as fertilizer in their potato fields.

After the Civil War, news started to spread about huge trophy brook trout being caught in the Rangeley

Lakes region of western Maine. They were crazy big—ten-plus pounds big. By the early 1900's anglers were coming from far and wide to fish for them. And fish they did. They fished like Hell and that might have been alright, but man is in a constant battle with himself and usually nature pays the price. We couldn't leave the lakes alone. Since the brook trout fishing was world class, some folks thought it would be a good idea to "improve" the fishery even more, so landlocked salmon and smelt were introduced. As it turns out, the huge brook trout were not some mutant strain of fish like something from an Arthur Conan Doyle novel. They were big because of the Blueback trout populations in the lakes. That, and the remoteness of the region. The Bluebacks were forage for the brookies. After a few generations of the added angling pressure and the added predation from the salmon, the Bluebacks were gone from the Rangeley Lakes forever. So are the mutant brook trout.

While native Bluebacks once populated freshwater ponds and lakes throughout Northern New England and Maritime Canada, now they're found in only nine different bodies of water in the world—all in Maine. (There is only one pond in Maine with Sunapee trout, and there is an established population of Bluebacks in Sawtooth Lake in Idaho from a stocking program many years ago.) Being a Maine native myself I just had to catch one.

With all this information there was nothing left to do but go fishing. So my father-in-law Dick and I threw the Tripper atop my beat-up Chevy truck and headed northwest toward one of the ponds on the list of blueback fisheries. We hit the road – literally. With the bottom of the truck over what seemed like a thousand miles of dirt roads with frost heaves the size of Volkswagens. Some of the heaves were marked with alder branches stuck in the ground, leaning toward the center of the road with a piece of red or orange cloth tied to it. These are traditionally placed fifty to 100 yards on either side of the heave to warn the "motorists." It occurred to us after a while that Canadian tradition (we were on the border), was to place the alder flags directly on top of the heave, leaving no real warning. That would be fine if you know which tradition you were following. Some were marked one way, some "tuther" and we hit them pretty hard. We got some air a couple of times. It was nerve-wracking.

When we finally got to the pond, the only camping spot was only a few yards from a dead moose calf. We pontificated for a while as to which way the prevailing winds were likely to blow from, then set camp. It wasn't too long before we had the canoe in the water. We paddled out of the cove past a cow moose feeding

100 yards from us in about four feet of water. The beautiful pond is one of Maine's thousands. The shoreline is choked from all sides with spruce and fir trees, intermingled with stands of cedars leaning out from the undercut banks as if they are trying to blanket the water...to hold it back from over-flowing.

It was the end of June and, as usual, the first order of business was what fly to start with. Like brookies, Bluebacks are opportunists, and will eat almost anything when feeding. A hundred years ago the method anglers used to fish for these guys was to plug fish. In those days that meant putting a little piece of raw lobster meat on a hook and jig near the bottom. That was back in the day when lobster was considered to be "poor man's food." The lobsters (to this day called "Bugs" Downeast, by those that fish for them), were sort of trashy and people gathered them up off the shore at low tide to use as fertilizer (like the Bluebacks). I guess folks just couldn't get enough stuff to make their gardens grow. Nowadays bait fishermen use worms instead of lobster, so there is almost no temptation to boil and eat your bait if the fishing is slow. But I'm a fly fisherman...and can't say with authority what bait fishermen might do when the fishing is slow.

I had a couple of rods with me, and started with a little three-weight Loomis, which was my favorite for years until I stumbled and snapped it in half one day.

I may have cursed. I've never had the money to replace it. But on that day it was intact as I casted to shore, off points, and in the coves under the cut banks while holding the canoe just off of one of the inlets. Nothing. I tried Elk Hair Caddis, Hoppers, Muddlers, and Woolly Buggers. I remember standing in the canoe, casting. Dick was content and recumbent in the bow of the boat, hands folded on his chest puffing on his cigar. I thought, well, I can keep flailing and hope that one mentally impaired trout would defy his nature and be cruising the shallow water, "looking up" on a warm late afternoon, or, I could listen to the fisheries biologist and world-class charr expert. "Lake trout like habits," Mr. Kircheis told me. So I changed tactics.

We could read the slopes of the hills that fell into the pond on either side. We found the biggest inlet and knew where the outlet was. It was pretty easy to guess where the deepest channel in the pond was. Down went the three-weight and up went the five-weight, with a sink-tip line. I could only hope to get the fly about ten feet down with a four-foot, lead-core header looped between the sink-tip and the leader. Dick and I both paddled. I wedged the rod under the bend of my right knee, the line trailing behind us about 120 feet. We tried a small nine-three, a black ghost and a pink lady. Not even a strike. After a while, I tied on a number 8 marabou black ghost and in no longer than the time it took to pay out the line again, we had a strike. I missed him, but he came back in an instant and hit it again...this time I got him with a gentle hook set. He thrashed around like a brook trout, then tried to sound like a lake trout. When we boated him, I couldn't help but think he seemed kind of delicate...he was so slender and a good sized male just over eleven inches. These fish have the potential to live twenty years and can grow to twenty-four inches, but you're much more likely to catch one six to ten inches. For equal length they are thinner than brookies. It was painful to kill him, but we did, and whereas I could not eat him, the honor fell to Dick. He said it was better than brook trout. Kircheis mentioned the same thing when he remarked that in places around the world, where arctic charr is legally sold commercially, it commands a higher price than salmon.

The grazing cow moose was gone when we paddled back into the cove to the campsite. The dead one was still there. We only had time to fish that afternoon and evening. We had a long drive home in the morning, with a great many frost heaves to negotiate. As the fire died and we got ready to hit the hay (goose down, actually), we made plans to come back in early spring next year when the Bluebacks would be nearer the surface. Now that one fish was tasted, it would be catch-and-release from here on out.

Underdogs without a doubt, Bluebacks are fish that have been beat up on over the last 100 years, with most of their home waters taken from them. Still, they're a tough fish, and I think if they could complain, they wouldn't. They're much harder to catch on a fly than my other favorite underdog, the Grayling, and they deserve a spot on so many eastern fly fishers bucket list. I realize I'm damned lucky to live in Maine for a lot of reasons, and I fully appreciate how fortunate I am to fish for Bluebacks every spring. Although I've caught scores of them, they'll never be scratched off *my* bucket list...they'll always be right up there with Halle Berry and witnessing a miracle.

Urubamba Dreamin'

Blue Hill, 2009

I first met Alberto Miori in 1986 in Cuzco, Peru one chilly morning while on my way out of town, heading to the fortress city of Ollantaytambo. I immediately knew there was something different about him. A forty-year-old climber, he was taller than most of the Quechua locals. I could also tell there was something about him that was different from the many touristas in town. Very fit and handsome as Hell, he had an air of confidence (but not over-confident) and intelligence. He looked like a super-in-shape Desi Arnez.

We were to meet up with some trekkers and accompany them along the Inca Trail into Machu Picchu...one of the greatest walks in the world. The Inca Trail is one of the old "roads" the Inca used 500 years ago, networking throughout their empire. It was their networking, organizational skills and communication that made the Incan Empire such a success for so long.

I liked Alberto right away. He was born and raised in Argentina, had lived in the U.S. for a while and traveled throughout South America before settling in Cuzco. At the Cross Keys pub the night before we left for the trek, we drank pisco sours, played darts and he told me when he lived in the States, he worked for a while for the Bureau of Land Management counting wild burros in the Grand Canyon. A few more piscos (VERY potent cocktails) under our belts, he told me what a great job that had been. But he was pretty sure that he was just counting the same few individual animals over and over again and felt a little bad about that. He just shrugged his shoulders and said, "How could one tell?"

We gathered up the trekkers in the morning, herded them onto a bus and were off to Ollantaytambo (pronounced; oh-YAN-tay-TAAM-bow).

There are many archaeology sites all over Peru, Machu Picchu being the most famous. But the old fortress city of Ollantaytambo is one of the finest examples of Incan engineering. Located near the head of the famous Sacred Valley of the Incas, about sixty miles from Cuzco, the city is the most popular start of the three to five day hike on the Inca Trail to Machu Picchu. People still live in dwellings made by ancient Incas. I never got tired of just walking among the temples, fountains and simple dwellings, or climbing up to the many terraces and fortifications, or to the many storehouses clinging to the steep hillsides.

There are lots of theories of how the Inca built such huge, amazing structures (the wheel was unknown to them). I don't know that much about it, but I don't think there are many cultures around today who would put in the same effort with the same attention to detail. They used no mortar, yet as modern buildings collapse during frequent earthquakes in Peru, the walls of the old Inca structures remain standing. You can't slip a dollar bill into the joinery. If you go there, which I highly recommend, you'll certainly be moved...unless you're crazy, or have lost your soul somewhere in Lima, which can actually happen.

It was in Ollantaytambo that the last great Incan leader, Manco Inca, made his last stand against the Spaniards during the conquest of Peru. He was the leader of the resistance at the time, and Alberto told me Manco was the only Inca to capture, and ride, one of the Conquistadore's horses.

The first night after setting up camp just outside of town, I wasn't long rigging the fly rod and picking my way through the planted fields to the Urubamba River. The farmers looked toward me more with curiosity than disdain. In Montana, I never got used to the rich folks making such a big deal of denying access to great fly fishing waters. But there I went, in the Sacred Valley of the Incas, carefully walking through people's back yards and all that was required was a friendly smile and a wave. I'm a landowner also, and wouldn't deny access to the stream along the back of the lot. It's pretty well known that flyfishers, specifically, are typically very respectful of people's property. And they never litter.

Unless you're fishing one of the many tributary streams which feed the Urubamba, the difficulty lies in negotiating the steep banks and cliffs, in many spots. I can be remarkably gommy (Maine speak for uncoordinated) and a simple ankle fracture in the remotest parts of South America can be accompanied by a unique set of complications...so I was overly careful. When I finally reached the river bank, I found a stick and wedged it into the rocks, poking out over the water a bit and tied a red bandana to it. I changed out of my Merrill hiking boots and into the Teva sandals and placed the boots on a flat rock under the stick. The Tevas were a little slippery, but the best things I had for wading. Wading in the water is no problem in many parts of Peru, certainly not here in the mountains. In the Manus, there are piranha, but they don't really bother you like in the old movies, when schools of piranha would devour cows and hapless porters whole, bones and all. In Venezuela, I saw a candiru, a tiny, skinny fish that reportedly will, if you pee in the water, swim up your urethra. It has retrose spines along its body and gets lodged in the penis. The pain, I've been told, is remarkable. The fish (with some damage to the penis) has to be surgically removed. When I first heard about the fish, I thought, that would be a great fish to catch and knock off the bucket list. But over the years I've grown fond of my apparatus and didn't think it would be wise to use it as bait. I'm happy, nowadays, for that transient moment of common sense, during a period in my life when if something was fraught with danger, it was worth doing.

The wading danger in the Urubamba is that it can be a torrential class 5 river the further downstream you go, especially later in the year. But this was June, and where I chose to fish was pocket water...about 80 yards across. There were no trees lining the river's edge, just some pretty little bushes that looked like miniature paloverde trees interspersed with short bushes resembling big lavender plants. Perfect fly-catchers for the back-casts of a below average caster.

I stepped out over some bleached-out pieces of drift wood and tried to step on boulders that wouldn't shift under my 180 pounds. I could see a long, deep bend pool slightly upriver from where I stumbled out onto the bank and tried to make my way to the tail of it. The most frustrating part, for me, of fishing new rivers in areas of the world where nobody else fly fishes (sometimes, where nobody else has *ever* fly fished) is what fly to start with. It's hard enough to choose back home, on familiar waters. In the highland streams and rivers of Peru, it was either streamers or big nymphs. According to my journal, I tied on a size 8 variation of a March Brown nymph, only because I had seen some medium-size light brown flies flying by while we were setting up camp an hour earlier. I often tied flies with whatever I could find while traveling in those days. The dubbing was from an alpaca in Cuzco, the tail was from a really cool feather I'd found while hiking (not from a pheasant) and the legs were feathers from these really neat chickens this old lady had with her at the Sunday market in Pisac a week before. My Quechua being weak, I'm not exactly sure what I did say to the chicken woman (I think I actually *did* call her "chicken woman") who undoubtedly thought I wanted to buy a whole live bird from her. I'd like to describe the look on her face when I gave her three U.S. dollars—a lot for a chicken—and just plucked a few feathers from under the wing and handed the bird back to her unharmed...but I can't.

On my first cast, about a third of the way up into the bend pool, I missed what looked like a 16 or 18-inch rainbow. A couple of casts later I hooked and landed a much smaller trout. He was quite silvery, with only a hint of pink below the lateral line. I worked my way out into deeper water and found a spot where I could get a nice drift with only two small mends. It was one of those things. I stood right there and even though I was (and still am) an average fly fisherman, I caught a couple dozen trout. Some were big, 18 inches or more, some were small and some had more color. I could just cast, facing the pool, at 9 o'clock, 12 o'clock, 2 o'clock and so on. By the time I worked my way down river and landed a fish at the tail of the pool, it was as if the head of the pool was already rested. It was crazy. In the middle of it all I hooked a pretty heavy fish and broke the fly off. Here's the point...there are a crap load of fish in most of the highland rivers of Peru and most of those fish are pretty uneducated when it comes to artificial flies. If the trout at the Henry's Fork have PhD's, then the Peruvian trout are Special Ed. On the other hand, they are extremely strong from living in such heavy currents and seem to never stop fighting. As I got ready to quit, I noticed Alberto sitting in the grass above me, watching me fish between turning pages of a book. He'd seen fly fishing many times before in his travels, I'm sure, but he'd never tried it. Back at camp we settled into the usual great camp fare—cheap, beautiful Chilean Merlot, discussions about politics and about the Sendero Luminoso (the Shining Path Maoist terrorist group) and our individual travels and anecdotes. Many camp sites in the most popular parts of third-world countries are often used by several groups at a time. Germans, Italians, Canadians, Yanks (sometimes we who are from the States are called Yanks, rather than "Americans," in South America...they're Americans, too) even French, share the camp sites, and before you know it, there is a lot of diffusionism going on. Old tattered journals are produced and stories are swapped. Many times I found myself in conversations with other wandering, semi-confused and equally poor souls and I would often think the scene was not unlike others throughout the centuries along countless pilgrim trails, in smoky tents, folks from completely different walks of life passing along travel tips and the whereabouts of bandit hide-outs. Usually there were those weighing-in on whether or not they liked the taste of "que," roasted guinea pigs commonly eaten in Peru. The oily meat isn't too bad, but the rodents are typically not dressed out before cooking and the teeth and toenails in your plate take a little getting used to. Towards the end of the evening, someone produced a stoneware jug of chicha beer and passed it around. Chicha is made (as I understand it...I never explored it) by the local women chewing corn, spitting it into the jugs, adding river water and then burying it in the ground for long enough time to ferment. The most I could ever drink without getting "right sideways" was three glasses. Alberto started asking details about fly fishing. Being a smart, worldly-wise, romantic guy, in the morning before breakfast, he picked it up in a flash after his first cursory stream-side lesson...even caught a couple of trout, as I remember.

After Alberto left the river to get some supplies in town, I hiked up a nearby tributary called the Patacancha, a much smaller stream which tumbles down a hillside next to Ollantaytambo. The fishing was easy there. The banks cut into meadows on both sides, and except for the steepness, it resembled a Wyoming spring creek I know. The casting was simple and the rainbows held in the quick water and took nymphs hungrily. There was a small campesino (farmer) boy watching and I killed three or four trout and gave them to him. He strung them on a stick, just like I did back home in Maine when I was his age, then ran home, excited. For a long time after that, whenever I returned to Ollantaytambo, the Patacancha was the first place Sweetness and I visited. Sweetness was, of course, my Sage fly rod, and I say *was*, because a few years ago I broke her and now Sage rods are out of my price range. But, we had a good run, catching fish on four continents.

The fireside chats, as I said, often turned to the Sendero Luminoso. Started by a college professor of philosophy back in the late 1970's named Abimael Guzman, they were said to have murdered thousands back in the eighties. I was in Peru a lot during the eighties and I couldn't substantiate that. Although I did hear a lot of stories about Senderos molesting travelers, most of their attacks were against police, the military and government officials. Their aim was to create a worker's state like Mao Tse Tung's China. They hated the United States *and* the Soviet Union. There was one incident near Kilometer 88 (a train stop along the Inca Trail between Ollantaytambo and Machu Picchu) which I know to be true. A group of Europeans escaped physical harm when the Sendero stole their money, passports, clothes, and camping gear. They walked on in their undies. I know it's true because I gave some clothes to a Finn in the group.

The only two times that I encountered the Senderos, that I was aware of, I happened to be fishing. Except for their posturing, they didn't appear any different than any of the other local young adults. Both times the small group of men stood high on the nearby stream bank and watched me cast for a while, then were gone. I like to think the poetry of fly fishing, the sheer beauty of the hand and rod working in concert, the line flowing behind, then forward and delivering the fly in just the right spot moved them like it does so many people. The loveliness of the art weighed upon them and they realized the errors of their ways, and that maybe they could live after all with a responsible capitalism married with social accountability, and they ran home and tore down their posters of Mao. Or not. They probably simply weren't interested in me, or my fly rod, and they likely figured they couldn't sell the rod, and that wading the stream I wouldn't have brought all my money with me in the event that it could get wet.

Friends tell me that since the arrest of Guzeman in 1992, the guerillas have splintered and are less active. One friend told me that what's left of the Senderos have become organized drug traffickers. I don't know...I'm just glad we don't have to deal with stuff like that when we fish brooks in Maine or Montana mountain streams. Guerilla organizations or obnoxious access-denying landowner lobbyists...we all have our obstructionists in life, some bigger than others.

The best fishing I found around Ollantaytambo (Ollantay, locally) was further to the south, upriver, especially in some of the streams where they feed into the Urubamba. The streams in the Sacred Valley make their way through corn and potato fields and along countless terraced fields filled with other plantings. Camp sites can be found amidst the groves of eucalyptus trees that line the valley on either side of the rivers. The most productive water in any of the highland streams and rivers are in the bend pools, or in the large pools above a naturally occurring falls. Called "lagoons" by the locals, there are quite a few the farther you can get upstream. I found many lagoons up the Rio Apurimac, about fifty miles from Cuzco. Closer inspection of some of the "naturally occurring" obstructions revealed worked stones, as if they were placed there hundreds of years ago...perhaps to create a place in the river where casting a net would be easier.

The trail to Machu Picchu is gradual and pleasant. A hiker passes through a transition from upland steppes, through cloud forests, to jungle. Hiking the Inca Trail, instead of taking the train, allows the traveler to bypass Aguas Calientes, a town about a mile before the gates to Machu Picchu. It's a pretty town at times but in winter it can be a little dismal, without much grass but with a lot of mud.

Machu Picchu can get under your skin and really grease your imagination. It's one of the most fabled locations on the planet. Dozens of roofless houses, shrines and courtyards in perfect condition atop a spectacular hilltop, playing host these days to daily insults by hoards of international tourists. Still, it's not hard to get some separation from the crowd to meditate and contemplate your own personal essence (and *then* existence)...if you're into that kind of thing, and, from what I saw in the dozen-or-so times I was there, a lot of folks do just that. If you're not into that, it's a better place to people-watch than the terminal at JFK. One of my favorite individuals of all time to watch was the gatekeeper. While a lot of locals were mestizo, half white blood, half Indian blood, the gatekeeper was all Indian. Old and wizened, he looked at each tourista as if he was overcoming bad cataracts, his sunken eyes deep in his leathery face. More likely he was sizing people up...hoping to find people in the line who will embrace the spirit of the place. Show some respect. I spent some time getting to know him on the second trip to the ruins. I was respectful, and on subsequent trips he would let me in after dark to wander among the stones in the moonlight. I know that on occasions he would let other gringos in at night, but by myself or with the right people, it was magical. I never saw any ghosts, or even anything unexplainable, but I did see unspeakable beauty...every time.

The ruins are at about 9,000 feet above sea level, and we often arrived there after a quick trip from Lima, so altitude sickness was always a concern. It was at Machu Picchu that I first tried to treat the symptoms with the local recipe, coca leaves. The headaches, nausea and depression from the altitude sickness, which the locals call *soroche,* can be debilitating. Almost everyone over the age of eighteen who lives in the Peruvian mountain regions chews coca. They keep a wad tucked into their cheek like a 1970's National League baseball player. Swallowing the thick green saliva alleviates thirst, hunger, cold, and fatigue. The coca leaves, from which cocaine is derived, is cultivated on the warm eastern slopes of the Andes. *Erythroxylon coca* leaves are picked four different times during the year, sun-dried and then shade-dried to retain the green color. Alberto told me that coca leaves were chewed by the Incas, but the legend says only by royalty or priests. Each time I tried it, I hated it. It was bitter as hell and didn't seem to help at all. I was probably not holding my mouth right.

I never got to explore the fly fishing around Machu Picchu much because by the time I got there I was well into the adventure travel guide role. One morning after the gatekeeper had allowed a late night stroll, I was sitting upon one of the terraces in the heart of the ruins, soaking up the warm sun, reading Jim Bartles' guide book of the Cordillera Blanca. As the tourists filed by, awed by the beautifully polished monoliths, I was suddenly overcome by intense pain near my groin. I leapt up with a shriek (that's right...I occasionally shriek), pulled my shorts down past my knees and started pounding away at my nether-region with my hands. Violently. It took a few moments to realize I had been stung twice by a small beige-colored scorpion *very* close to my peenie. It really, really hurt. I adjusted my linens, pulled my shorts back up and composed myself. The tourists had given me a wide berth. I had killed the scorpion and scooped it up into an empty film canister. I wasn't being disrespectful, honest. Unfortunately, I looked up and saw the gatekeeper watching me from 100 feet away, backlit by the sun, his hands clasped behind his back. He never let me in at night again.

Seasons End

Pleasant River Lake, September 2009

In Maine, September is the finest month for a lot of us. While we will often have wet, cold springs and notoriously short summers (this summer it seemed to rain almost every day), Septembers usually have bright, blue skies, warm days, and cool nights. The black flies and the mosquitoes are distant memories, and the traffic onto and off Mount Dessert Island is doable again. The tourists have petered out and the locals can breathe a collective sigh of relief. It's not that Mainers don't appreciate tourism...it's just that at this time of year we can actually run to the store for more duct tape without having to plan ahead.

It's hard to tell if the average Mainer is really tuned in to how much tourism contributes to Maine's economic development and stability. But it *is* fun to watch for license plates, read the funny bumper stickers and it's a kick to guess the wacky accents. Without the tourists we would miss being in line at Walmart and nudging the wife, whispering, "yup...they're from Jersey. No way...New York."

More importantly, the conditions for fishing are nearly perfect in September. The brook trout are pre-spawn, so the males get aggressive and are spectacularly red bellied. The salmon are moving into the rivers in big numbers and are stacking up in the pools. There are still some good caddis hatches and caddis emerger imitations work great in September. Every fall, my friend Dave Dumas insists on fishing humongous, florescent-pink San Juan worms in the Allagash. They're ugly, the idea of it is ugly, and he will stand in one spot at the head of a pool for half an hour and catch brookies with almost every cast. Last year I gave in and tried one for a few minutes. I did catch a couple, but it seemed like cheating a little bit so I switched back to a parachute wolf with a #16 caddis emerger dropper. I caught just as many fish (as many as *I* had been...not as many as Dave did) and I felt good and pure again. I have no problem with fishing the pink uglies in New Mexico, but they seem out of place in the Allagash. It's my problem...I'll get over it. My son, at the age of fourteen, is already a dry fly purist through and through, so there's no worry of him becoming a pink-worm, cheater-fly fisherman.

Every September, a few of us rent one of the Macannamac camps in the north Maine woods. Some of the guys have known each other since the third grade and a few of them have made the trip twenty-five years in a row. The good part of hanging out with guys like that is they become like family. You can count on each other to no end and the comfort level is always the highest. On the other hand, the *bad* part of hanging out with guys like that is they become like family...they're the first to put you in your place and there is no bullshitting them. It's awesome.

We typically fish the West Branch of the Penobscot for landlocks as a stop-over on the way up to camp (in Maine, pronounced "upta" camp). Once there, we fish several of the small ponds near the lodge along with a couple of trips to the Allagash. It's a special trip for me personally because my favorite salmon fishing is the West Branch and my favorite brook trout fishing is the Allagash.

The West Branch is a bona fide, internationally known salmon fishery. It's big and can be a little scary to wade. It has big water, big salmon, big trout, and big caddis and stonefly hatches. It's the only river in Maine I know of where a competent fly fisher stands at least a chance of catching a seven pound fish in fast, heavy water. I never have, but then again I don't think anybody classifies me as competent. In my experience, the best fishing is between Ripogenus Dam at the outlet of Chesuncook Lake and just below a long, deep run called The Big Eddy further down river. Probably the very best water is directly below the dam where the river gouges its way through a deep gorge. In the gorge, it is inaccessible in most spots from water's edge, and I don't have a raft so I've never been able to fish it. Below the gorge, the river settles down into a series of falls, runs, drops, and class three and four rapids. Just about all of the wadeable sections hold fish. Starting in April and continuing through October, at 9:10 a.m. each day, there is a caddis hatch which cools off around 11:30 a.m. There are mayfly hatches throughout the spring and early summer and stonefly nymphs are productive, but it is the caddis flies on this river that are (to me) most important. Some anglers make the trip with nothing but stoneflies. All trout fly fishers love the mayfly, and so do trout, but as the years go by I believe the caddis is a far more important food source for fish than most people think. (It's well accepted that caddis are a close second to mayflies.)

Unlike mayflies, caddis flies have a larval stage that trout will feed on. Some larvae are free living, dwelling with the mayfly nymphs among the rocks on the stream bed. They resemble grub-like worms with tiny legs three on each side near the front of the body and hooks on their butts to grip things with, but most caddis larvae build cases made from sticks or gravel to live in. If you've ever pumped a trout or salmon's stomach, sometimes you'll see that fish feed on these also...cases and all. Caddis emergence is often at dusk or well into the night, but as I said, at the West Branch, it seems to be mid to late morning.

Caddis hatches are not as concentrated as mayflies and adult caddis flies are hard to observe in the air. At times, they might not be hatching at all but rather returning to the water to deposit their eggs. But once you figure out a particular stream or river, you'll know which stage to fish, and when. Since caddis hatches are more sporadic (plus the addition of the larval stage) and trout seem to feed on them more randomly, matching the hatch isn't always the foremost component to your presentation. I think that makes caddis and caddis emerger (pupa), or larvae imitations, the best searching patterns to try when not much is happening on the water or in the air.

There are hundreds of species of caddis flies and some are quite varied physically. It's a good idea if you can capture one in your hat and examine it. It's amazing how varied they can be in waters just miles apart. I can tell you that the predominant fly at the West Branch is a case-builder, a medium-brown to dark fly with tent-like wings that lie a little flatter on the body than some other species. On the Allagash River, just to the north, I've found a lot of free-living larvae, which is probably why Dave's San Juan Worm works for him.

The larval stage of the case-building caddis is remarkable. Once the little, defenseless grub-like thing hatches, it goes about doing what it has to do for any chance of survival. It builds a fort around itself. The most common cases you'll find under and between rocks in a stream bed are made up of either sticks or other types of vegetation, or of sand pebbles. Some are a combination of whatever they can find in their immediate environment. A friend of mine once told me he found a caddis case made partially out of a cigarette filter. That is both disgusting and amazing. The cases, from an engineering standpoint, make beaver lodges (beaver *houses*, in Maine) look like thrown together outhouses. As you might guess, the cases are held together with glue-like saliva...super spittle, if you will. Some species simply increase the size of their "house" as they increase in size, some shuck the case and gather materials to build a new case (called molts, or instars), at which time they are quite vulnerable to the hungry fish.

There is a third form of caddis larvae. These are net builders and act a bit like underwater spiders. These larvae use the super spittle to construct silky nets attached to the bottom of the stream or river in a position to filter food from the natural flow of the water. For years I nymphed the West Branch with #18 to #22 pheasant tails and had consistent success. On one trip there in 2009, my friend Jeff

Sheff had me try a #18 green caddis pupa with a dark bead head, olive body, a little peacock herl behind the bead, and two tiny emerger-type wings of clipped duck wing poking out from under the herl. It was as if the inner dome of Heaven had opened up! That's what the salmon wanted alright. I've used that fly there ever since and have caught fish every time. My boy, Hazen, fished the West Branch for the first time last September on the way upta camp and hooked his first salmon on a fly, with his first cast, using that same caddis pupal pattern. I screwed up the netting of his fish but it didn't seem to matter. He played it beautifully into slack water at his feet, it flipped out of the net and she broke off. We were going to release her anyway...but a photo would have been nice, although I did snap some pictures of him playing it. Earlier that spring, on the opposite bank of the river, I did the same thing to another friend, Tom Crowe, who had hooked the biggest brook trout I've seen in Maine. I had it in the net for a millisecond and the tail and head both protruded out of the ends of my oval net. He was a twenty-plus-inch male with a kyped jaw. Maybe there's an online netting course I could take.

There's a dichotomy of folks that go to that same fishing camp each fall, friends that are like brothers...and some are actually real brothers. We have a pile of Nasberg's from Bangor that are part of the group (or should I say we have Nasbergs that have piles) and one of them, Jerry, owns one of the famous Pat's Pizza restaurants in Maine and is, at least, a national-class chef. We don't eat crap upta camp. Great, hearty breakfasts and every supper is a camp wonder...cuisines from around the world. Everyone relaxes and cuts loose, and before he was eleven, my son could recite one (and pretty much only) camp rule..."What's said at fishing camp, stays at fishing camp."

The end of the week at fall fishing camp is sad because it's a harbinger of the end of the regular open water fishing season. I try to spread out the last few weekend trips throughout the state...one more to the north country, striper fishing if they came up the coast far enough, and some fall browns in the St. George River near Appleton. There is some nice October catch-and-release fishing to be had for salmon in places like the east outlet of the Kennebec or the Roach River, which is fine because we mostly release our fish anyway. I kill a few trout every year and maybe two salmon annually to eat, and I don't feel one bit bad about it. I never seem to fish much in October, with all the pre-winter chores to do. Just putting-up firewood occupies a couple of weekends. The firewood should have been done the previous spring, I know, but I'm not about to cut and stack firewood during a Hendrickson hatch.

The end of fly fishing season isn't too painful. There is the house winterizing to finish (a big deal in Maine), a little hunting to do, put the garden and the bees to bed, etc. My father used to say, "There are two seasons in Maine...winter (pause with a tired look here), and getting ready for winter." By January, I'm tying flies in earnest and the cuts in my fingers from leaders have all healed. By early February, I'm reorganizing all the gear, planning out the first few trips of the year and coming up with a wish list of the more ambitious excursions. As the winter trudges on, I start the real daydreaming and I'll read through my old journals from my younger years, back when I had hair and opportunities up the ying-yang. I'm obviously not a trained writer and so the journals are just so-so (sophomoric and painful to read, really). But when reading my notes about fly fishing places like the Sea of Galilee, the Amazon, the River Dee or the Arctic, my memories augment the missing pieces in the journals.

Northern Maine in the dead of winter can be a trying time, and not just for fly fishers. Reading the old journals reminds me of the sights and smells, the fish I caught and lost and the friends I made around the world...some of whom died way too young. I turned fifty this year and some of the details of the memories are harder to come by, becoming opaque, like the lenses in my eyes. When my final fishing season ends, my children will have the journals, damning as they may be, if I haven't lost them by then. They can read my essays if they're interested— although it's not *my* fishing memories that are important...but theirs. So I will keep dreaming up fishing trips, putting off chores and making great, fond, new memories in the minds of my kids. A gift is a gift, after all, and to me, the gift of fly fishing, together with the gifts of life or love, has to be the top three.

Little Waters

Otter Stream February, 2008

Growing up my summers were spent on, and in, a lake in Maine. The lake itself has become like an old friend, having long ago given up most of its secrets as if I was held in its trust. Every half submerged log, every drop-off and every beach unoccupied by a camp was familiar. All of the big boulders lining the shore that were worth diving off had names. The only island became the nucleus of the nine hundred and eight acre living organism. There were only two good-sized brooks that filled the lake along with two other smaller brooks which were small enough to jump across in mid-summer. My father and some friends built a camp there when I was three, where we spent weeks every summer. While the lake was home to all of us, the brooks, to me, became exotic, interesting destinations of adventure and exploration. Forty years later, all brooks and small streams by association are still held fondly in my heart, maybe more so as the years go by.

To a small boy the brooks seemed mysterious. What secrets were around each bend? What fish lived there? How big were they? Where were the hobos and Indians that surely lived along the brook? Were they watching my every move from the dark cedars? Those lampreys that showed up one summer...did they come straight from Hell, like it seemed? The more bends in the brooks I explored the further I got from the lake...and from the safety of camp. Yet, enough trips up a brook and one may really know it. The big river, the outlet, was too distant...too much an institution. The brook was small enough to be an individual...to be intimate. It became *friendly*. One brook near camp (technically a stream), held a lot of native brook trout. A couple of times each year, Dad and I would escape the women (no small feat...there were six or seven females at any one time) and make the short trip with lunch, wading clothes and worms packed into the old Chevy. We usually drove older cars, or at least that's what it seems like looking back. The most important criterion was that the car could seat about ten people, but this was before the encumbrance of seatbelts. Seven or eight siblings would often fight over who got to sit where...the back dash, the hump on the floor in the front or, me, being the youngest, whose lap would be the unfortunate recipient of my boney little ass for almost two hours? The routine seldom changed. The stream, where we fished it, ran for a couple of miles along the edge of some blueberry barrens. Dad would ease the old car over the boulders sticking up in the road. Then he would wrestle the Chevy (it was *always* a Chevy) into the bushes near the stream and park. We wore our wading clothes on the way in. We rigged up quickly; the creels, the rods and reels, extra hooks, spinners and swivels, and the worms. I can only remember my own rig—a five dollar Shakespeare rod and a Johnson Century reel. That was a great reel.

Dad was always second to get to the water and second to cast his line into the best pools. I always figured he was just a slow-poke, or simply not as excited to fish as me. As it turns out, I think he *was* excited. I didn't figure it out until many years later, when I would let my own son slip into the water first. When I would watch *him* almost shriek from the cold, cringe as the frigid water made its way to his testicles, and I would watch *him* get the first shot at the unsuspecting trout. Dad was no slow poke.

That particular stream still looks more beautiful than any other I've seen in Maine. It's a little more open along the shorelines than most and every bend looks like a calendar photo. Every 100 feet or so is a spectacular, trouty-looking pool. Even in those days, when the stream seemed full of trout, there were good catches and bad. It is hunger that impels the fish to take the bait and the hook takes him. The angler does the rest. We would usually keep a few fish, mostly for Mother. Brookies were a treat, for her.

It was on that stream that I saw my first Mayfly hatch, which can be magical to an adolescent fishing fanatic. Every flyfisher who puts pen to paper feels obligated to describe, define and explain the importance of the Mayfly. It has gotten to the point that I usually pass over any section of a book when the writer starts to pontificate about the insect. (Note to self: skip this paragraph.)

Mayflies (Ephemeroptera) are the most delicate and refined of all insects, period. Many common names have been thrust upon them and they have had more crimes laid on them than they could possibly bear. And there were billions of them to share the blame. A hatch, to the untrained eye, can be awesome. I've heard kids tell tall tales of getting stung or bitten by these gentle creatures. Fact is, no adult Mayfly ever stung or bit anything. Adult mayflies only live a day or two, three at most, so food is not important. Its mouthpart is vestigial and the whole adult aspect of its life cycle is dedicated to having sex—at least for the male Mayfly. One of the guys upta fishing camp is like that (you know who you are). As for the two or more appendages attached to their butt, well, they are useful to the owners but not as weapons. And these bugs are not built for speed. Their trembling, gauze-like wings and timid behavior make the Mayfly unquestionably likeable, once you know them well. They are damned lovely, actually. And apparently they taste good. Trout love them.

Mayflies are one of the four main trout stream insects, along with caddisflies, stoneflies and midges. Mayflies hatch from eggs which had been laid on the surface of the water, usually in small riffles in the evenings. They hatch out into nymphs and live most of their lives underwater. There are many types of Mayflies, but the typical life span is about one year. At the end of that year, the nymphs hatch by swimming to the surface of the water, where they shed their skins and sprout wings. The wings are often gray (*dun*-colored), which gives this stage of life its name...dun, as in pale-morning dun. Trout feed voraciously on these duns. If the insects escape, they fly to the trees and bushes to mature in a day or two. When ready, the Mayfly molts. Its wings become gauzy-clear and in most cases the body darkens. Then, the moment they've all been waiting for...they form into huge mating swarms over the stream, swirling and spinning overhead (in this stage they are called spinners) mating in mid-air in an entomologic orgy. I call it the twenty-foot high club. The females then lay their eggs on the water's surface. The beautiful, delicate Mayflies then lean over, dead (known as "spent"). The trout, salmon and other fish feed on the spent flies, with their perfect-looking wings spread flat on the surface. Yeah, that's what I saw on that stream in Maine, in the blueberry barrens when I was eleven.

Dragonflies have a somewhat similar life, although I think it takes at least a year and in some cases longer for them to mature. There comes a time for the nymph to leave the water and spend a few weeks in the air. The transformation takes place in warm weather, from spring 'til fall. Creeping from their watery home, compelled by some inner impulse, the young dragonfly climbs up a few feet from the water and gets a good grip on a stem or leaf of some water plant. If it can't find a good plant, it will use a stone, or even a piece of rubbish found in the water (if bait fishermen are around). While shedding the nymph skin and waiting for the wings to dry, it is quite helpless. It's crunch time. Out of its natural element, and not yet free from the armor which binds its wings, it falls an easy victim to insect-loving birds and other enemies. Extremely vulnerable...they must feel like they've just walked into the third grade classroom and—oh God...they're naked!

We've all seen the cast skins of dragonflies on the banks of streams, lakes or ponds. They're so life-like. I always have to look closely to see if they're empty. The next time you find one of the cast-off nymph skins of a damsel fly, or a dragonfly, remember Tennyson's wonderful lines:

"Today I saw the dragon-fly
Come from the well where he did lie;
An inner impulse rent the veil
Of his old husk; from head to tail
Came out clear plates of sapphire mail.
He dried his wings; like gauze they grew
Thro' crofts and pastures wet with dew
A living flash of light he flew."

One of the great things about fly fishing which separates that type of angling from spincast or bait fishing is the evolution aspect. (I don't mean fly fisher's themselves are more evolved...or *do* I?) I'm referring to the process of learning. One is constantly learning about the diet of the fish, fish biology, the life cycles of the food they eat, how weather affects different fish species, and how well do fish see, what color fly vest looks good on you, do trout always face upstream, do these waders make my butt look big— my God, the list goes on and on and the theories are ever changing. Evolution. No fly fisher on earth has ever learned everything about their sport (I don't know if fly fishing is really a sport unto itself...it's more like a life-partner). And no one on earth really knows the exact pronunciation of the Latin names of the insects that some fishermen love to throw around.

Dad and I never fished that stream for more than a couple of hours, working our way down stream until we hit some deadwater, then leaving the stream, we would cut across the barrens back to the car. The walk back was always uncomfortable...our clothes would be wet and heavy and the old worn-out sneakers that we saved to "wade the brook" were always full of sharp pebbles. Back at the Chevy we would change into our dry clothes. Dad was always on the opposite side of the car for modesty. Then we would sit by the stream where we started from and eat lunch.

My father was no master fisherman, but he knew a lot about the natural world. I listened and learned enough to catch fish in most situations, although today I'd have to rate my fly fishing abilities somewhere between crappy and fair.

I've been lucky enough to fish most of the world's largest rivers, and they're great. But it was along the small brooks, creeks and streams of Maine I think I learned the most. I carried a notebook when quite young and would jot down things to look up later on. Things like, "How the heck do gills work?" and "How do insects breath?" The gills are interesting. It's obvious that aquatic animals must be provided with special organs for obtaining air. The gills of fish are a complicated network of blood vessels, with very thin walls. The water of the brook, lake or river contains a lot of air—more than I thought. Every breeze that ripples the surface, every waterfall that churns the stream into foam, every drop of rain that strikes the water adds to its supply of air. The gills of the fish are constructed in such a way as to expose the surface to the air and water mixture. See there? Evolution. One of many tidbits to help one locate trout.

Pretty simple stuff, I know...but added up, everything you can pick up about the bio-diversity of a trout stream helps you to become a productive fly fisher. In Northern New England, even if you're not an angler, you would have to be a heartless bastard to remain unmoved by the beauty of those emerald green or indigo blue Damselflies flitting around in the filtered sunlight next to every brook where it finds its way through spruce and cedar forests, or the cardinal red Lobelia growing right out of the boulders that jut from the water.

To this day I'm drawn to smaller waters. I don't know if sitting on their banks helps me revisit old haunts, or if they appeal to me in some weird, psycho-metaphysical way, but I love a small brook. It's even better if the brook is in a wild place, and better still if there are trout in it. And best of all if they are small trout, and I have a 2-weight cane fly rod in my hand.

Home Waters

Bradley, Maine 2007

Home waters are waters quite near home, and are fished often when you can't get anywhere else and over time, they become intimate—like friends, or better.

The stream that borders the back of our property is sixty-five paces from our back door and forty-two paces from the end of our driveway (*dooryard*, in Maine). Ours was one of the original few farms in the town. The house and barn were built in the 1830's and it's likely the stream was the main water source for the entire farm. A quick stumble down the steep gully to the stream and you see a wide pile of boulders and smaller rocks strewn across the water to the other side, remnants of an old earthen dam. If you squint real hard, your eye can follow the lay of the land beyond the boulders and see the folks who came before once used the dam to cross over to the farm fields on the far banks. Squint harder and you can imagine what the fields used to look like on the far side of the stream, dotted now with homes, barns and patches of fields and woods.

What's left of the old dam still functions and holds back a small pool. It's not deep...in the summer the deepest sounding I've done is twelve feet, nine inches, but most of the main channel is more like seven feet. The pool is 140 yards long from head-to-tail and fifty-two yards at its widest spot. There are a few cedars, but mostly the banks are appointed with maples, elms and alders, along with a few ancient apple trees still hanging on from the farm days.

Otter Stream drains the wetlands of Sunkhaze Meadows that is part of Sunkhaze Meadows National Wildlife Refuge. When it leaves the meadows, it cuts through the back of the town of Milford and then winds its way through the middle of Bradley before dumping into the Penobscot River. It courses in front of the elementary school, behind the redemption center and then it slips under Main Street only about sixty yards from its confluence with the river. (A note about the redemption center: I once went in there without any cans or bottles and said to the fellow, "I feel bad about the way I sometimes treated my sisters in my youth." He stared at me for a moment and then, without missing a beat, he told me that I should call them and tell them how I feel. We both laughed and he said, "Redemption can be a funny thing.")

I first fished the stream during a work break, about three days after we bought the place. It was August and I took my Loomis three-weight with a (#18) green Joe's hopper. After about twenty sunfish, mostly pumpkinseed, and five or six with red breasts, I went back to the massive remodeling project at hand. Over the years we got to know the pond, as I say, intimately. We know that at times there are the two kinds of sunfish, smallmouth bass, pickerel, and I swear one summer I caught a good-sized black crappie on an elk-hair caddis. I didn't have a camera with me, but that's what it looked like. Early one spring, in the tailwater of the pond, I was nymphing for whatever would bite and was surprised to catch a little brookie. Pale, skinny and about six inches long, she looked lost and confused in water normally inhabited by warm water species. She might have come up from the Penobscot (unlikely) exploring, or (more likely), she had come downstream from the chain of tiny ponds up in the meadows some two miles away, which surely have some spring holes. Either way, she went back into the water even more confused.

That's the backyard. In front of the house and across the street is the Penobscot River. Famous for its Atlantic Salmon fishing of the past, the "lower" Penobscot is fished nowadays for smallmouth bass. There's nothing like hitting the Penobscot just right during the spawn, boating forty to fifty smallies with top-water flies and small poppers. It is great fun, and possibly *the* best way to teach a newbie how to cast, hook and play a fish on a fly rod.

Personally, I'd have to say the "upper" Penobscot with its landlocked salmon and big brook trout is more like one of my home waters. We fish it more often and the fish are *salmon*. Everyone who grew up fishing, either with their father, an uncle, a mentor, or whomever has a favorite fishing spot. Certainly, it is the memories, not the water, that make the place special, and that fondness and familiarity are what make it your "home water." It doesn't have to be forty-two paces from the dooryard.

In my memory, it's a stream in Beddington that is my favorite home water. It was a favorite place for my Dad to fish, and maybe that's why it's mine. I know every boulder in it and every bend pool. I know where the fish hold, year after year. To this day, I can stand with my feet in exactly the same spot where I caught my first big trout. It was fat bellied and fourteen-inches long, I was twelve years old and *not* fat bellied. And when I fish it these days, fifty years old and chock full of experience, I still feel Dad is there, saying something funny, and ready to grab the back of my shirt collar and haul me up if I stumble and start to go under. He was good at that. That's what "home water" is all about. Familiarity, memories and...love? Well, I do love the stream, and the memories that accompany it, and I love to go there every summer. In Maine you can hardly throw a cat without hitting a body of water. Many local fly fishers can walk from their home to wet a line. There are the favorites; The East Outlet, the Roach, Grand Lake Stream, the Pleasant, the West Branch, and the Allagash, but that little stream in the blueberry barrens in Beddington is for me, still number one.

When I lived in the Rocky Mountains, I used to fish for every kind of fish available in Montana, Colorado, Wyoming and Idaho. I thought perhaps I lived in a fly fisher's paradise. That's because I didn't know much of anything when I was in my twenties. Where I live now in northern Maine, and being somewhat wiser, I realize I'm much closer to paradise. The diversity of fishing is truly incredible. I can still fish for trout (rainbows, lake, splake, and browns), bass (both smallies and largemouth), charr (blueback and brook trout) pickerel, muskies, assorted panfish, white and yellow perch, salmon (Atlantic and landlocked) whitefish, *and* all the salt water species in the Gulf of Maine. (I'm going to say just one word...stripers.) I once watched biologists shock a small stream in Aroostook County to study what was living there. There was a total of sixteen species of fish.

If you're in a vehicle in Maine, you're never more than about ten minutes from fishable water of some kind, and less than a three hour drive to a prime trout or salmon fishery. Maine fishing is no big secret...the locals know it and it's the reason some of them live here. Fly fishers from the other New England states sure know it, as well as PA, NY, CT and well, all through the eastern United States. We get our share of anglers from out west. When I meet them, I wish I could hook them up with a couple of hard-core locals so they can really experience the amazing variety of fishing in the short time they are here.

On the other hand, these are home waters to some of us...do we *want* everyone to know?

Grand Lake Stream

Pleasant River Lake, July 2010

You might as well call Downeast Maine a mystical place. A lot of people talk about it, say they love it, even brag about it and joke about it, but nobody seems to know exactly where it is. There's even a magazine dedicated to the place, but in those pages everyone seems wealthy and all the homes cost millions. (Where I'm usually gated off.) To any Mainer who lives on the coast, Downeast starts at the southern edge of their own property and stretches north to Eastport. Ask someone from Portland and who knows what they'd say. Ask up in The County (Aroostook County, if the reader is from away) and they'll likely shrug their shoulders and say, with a wry smile and an inherent economy of words, "...it's not *here*." Like I said, nobody really knows where it is, but we Mainers know it exists. Like many things in the life of a Maine native, it is probably just a state of mind, like efficient State Government, or "wintering well." ("Wintering well" is actually doable by not getting sick, not dying, not running out of firewood, not getting impossibly in debt because of No. 2 heating oil, by keeping the pipes from freezing, not running the truck off the road, not getting pregnant (or impregnating someone), and avoiding frost bite after rolling the truck over.)

Originally Downeast wasn't a place. It was a direction dating back to when Maine wasn't even Maine...it was Massachusetts; we were a colony of a colony. A historical point that some Mainers still struggle with. (Mainers were fiercely independent then, as now, but deep down feel a certain unspoken kinship with folks from Mass. It's complicated.) In the old days when the sailing ships left Boston Harbor in a northeasterly course, they had the advantage of the prevailing westerlies, heading down east to Maine and to the Maritimes. Running "downhill," or "down east," which became a colloquialism that eventually evolved into Downeast. To this day if you're on the coast you say your "going *up* to Boston." It's a tidewater thing. If one is, let's say, forty miles inland, you use your gazetteer and say that you're "headin' down to Beantown."

From any part of the coast of Maine, if you go far enough Downeast (north, remember), you eventually leave the shore and (now you're "headin' north") find yourself driving through the town of Princeton and the Passamaquoddy Reservation. Slow down (trust me, the cops in Princeton are...vigilant) continue through the Rez, and if you are a fly fisher, hang a Louie onto the road that leads to Grand Lake Stream. GLS is part of the St. Croix River system, one of the four original systems to hold landlocked salmon populations. The St. Croix system includes West Grand Lake and Big Lake...both great fishing waters.

I have mixed feelings about fishing GLS every spring. It's pretty famous salmon water, holds fish on opening day (April 1st) and is productive...but it's often crowded as Hell. Most of the water we fish in Maine holds fairly considerate anglers. We try to share the pools when they're big enough, or let other fishermen try for a while. Some well-established fishin' holes, like the Bangor Salmon Pool, employ a rotation system...cast a few times, take a few steps. That way everyone present gets a shot at the holding fish. And there are stories of it being strictly enforced with expletives, pebbles and insults. During the first few weeks of April on Grand Lake Stream, without sharp elbows, it's an effort to find water to fish. It used to piss me off a bit, but after driving the two hours out the Airline (route 9) to get there one spring, I was in the parking lot at the dam pool, standing in the snow, changing out of my waders when I noticed the license plates...PA, NY, CT, NH, MA, and suddenly I couldn't blame the folks for camping out in the best spots. After all, I can get on the stream in any season. Although I suppose it could go both ways...the locals don't have to drive the long distance but they do have to endure the winter there. So they should have equal opportunity to fish, especially when the fishing is great.

The stream starts where it rips through the dam at West Grand Lake and flows for three-and-a-quarter miles where it meanders as quiet slack water into Big Lake. It's a pretty storied place for such a short stretch of water. If a place is to become "storied" then it needs a good bit of history and the town of Grand Lake Stream has seen its share of characters and celebrities. You'd be hard pressed to find any literature about GLS without seeing old photos of famous and semi-famous people lounging in the several guide lodges in the area lakes. Over the years, most of the famous fly fishing writers you've heard of have fished there, and you can't cast a fly without snagging someone who fished with (*the*) Ted Williams in the old days. The original American Sportsman, Curt Gowdy, filmed at least one episode of his weekly show there. Mr. Gowdy spent a fair amount of time on the stream and even had an old favorite spot just above the Cable Pool named after him. I wouldn't mind having a little point or even a rock named after me, but I'd probably have to drown for the notoriety and I'm fairly sure I'm not that dedicated. Without a doubt, GLS has always been one of the classic fly fishing destinations in Maine.

The town itself is a pretty cool place. The stream (it's actually a river) cuts right through the center of town and the way the streets are laid out (it was a tannery town), the river itself is "main street." You'll have to go there to feel it, but the first section of river and the town are one. The name of the town, Grand Lake Stream, is appropriate...one wouldn't exist without the other. That's a little corny, but at GLS it's actually true. Also, I don't know the numbers exactly, but I'm willing to bet that GLS has the greatest concentration of guides per capita in the country.

They say you never forget your first, and the first salmon I ever caught on a dry fly was at GLS. It was definitely a fluke, but I hooked and landed it anyway. In the first week of April, I drove down to meet-up with my mentor Chuck Green and his fishing partner Marty Arsenault. I had never been there. I found the town, parked in the wrong place, approached the river from the wrong side, waved to Chuck, tied-on the wrong fly, and made the wrong cast to the wrong water at the tail of the Dam Pool. In spite of all that, an eighteen-inch, skinny salmon (a *racer*) rose through the famous gin-clear water and ate my fly anyway. It was my first cast of the day.

By the time I netted and released him (or her) Chuck made his way over to me. When he inspected my #18 Hendrickson, he just shook his head and looked a little weirded-out. Apparently, nobody had caught a thing all morning. Later that night in one of the Canal Side Cabins Chuck explained there were very few hatches that early in April. One might rarely see a few Blue Winged Olives, but most fishermen used streamers or nymphs this time of year...so it was quite something that I caught one right on top. I wanted to apologize. He elaborated. Near opening day, there were either salmon that overwintered in the river, or those that made their way upstream from Big Lake to the dam. I don't believe there are any yellow perch in West Grand Lake, but there are in Big Lake, so when the salmon from downstream do start arriving in the river, Barnes Specials are a good bet. Chuck told me a schedule of the hatches I could expect over the next seven months. Off the top of his head, he spoke of the flying ants, the Hendricksons and the Red Quills of May and early June, and of the tan and black zebra caddis flies and the alder flies of July. Then he lovingly described the Blue Winged Olives of autumn. It was quite an education. Over the years I've developed what I call my "little black book," which is red. It's a compilation of flies that seem to work for me on many lakes, rivers, streams and brooks. At GLS, it's mostly bead-head caddis and pheasant tail nymphs. I've also caught a lot of salmon on #8 Lucky Chuck Specials, which are just weighted woolly buggers with a red head, olive body, brown hackle, and a black marabou tail. Don't ask...it just works.

A flow of less than 2,800 cubic feet per second, while not perfect is a good fishable amount of water. The controllers of the dam, Domtar, seem to make more effort than most corporations to control the flows in consideration of anglers and citizens who live downriver. They don't have to, but they do. In 2005, Maine had the wettest, coldest spring since the Civil War. We had over sixty inches of rain that year. My wife and I owned a nursery business at that time, and like other nurseries in the state, we could not keep many plants alive. We lost over 1,000 hanging baskets and tens of thousands of annuals. Eleven small nurseries in Maine went under that year. It was a tough year on fishermen also. Rivers and streams were swollen and flooded and some of the fisheries were in jeopardy. Several times that winter and spring the flow at the GLS dam was 4,000 cfs. The river didn't flood, per se, but it *was* rip-roaring. I returned to GLS a few years later and found the dam pool had changed significantly. In many spots where you couldn't wade before (too dangerous or too deep), you now could. In fact, after fishing the river for more than twenty years, I had to re-learn much of it, which of course, is half the fun.

There are the well known pools as you go downriver from the Dam Pool...the Hatchery, the

Evening, the Glide, Gowdy's Point, and the Cable Pool are some of the more popular ones. There are others, but those are the ones I'm most familiar with. The Glide and the Hatchery Pools are my favorites. They're beautiful, productive and, as I am unencumbered with talent, I can cast well enough to fish them. Both pools are fairly straightforward casting and wading.

The Pine Tree Store (the only game in town) is just as well known as any of the pools. It's a jewel in Maine. The owners, Kurt and Kathy Cressey, are remarkably helpful and pleasant to all fishermen. They are patient and friendly beyond all reason. I don't know how many times, after getting skunked once again, I sat on the bench in front of the store and watched the town go by. It went by slowly. The store is certainly not a miracle of supply, but it's got everything (everything important to life, anyway), beer, pizza, coffee, and fly fishing tackle.

We all have our reasons why we fish and often those of fly anglers coalesce a bit more than other outdoor men and women. You might not speak to another fly rodder on the water, but usually there is fraternization of a high order going on. Fly fishers share the same intense love of the fish, the same quest for knowledge, the same sense of history and of preservation, and occasionally the same conceits.

Grand Lake Stream is not my favorite place to fish. My favorites are generally smaller waters where my Dad and I fished together, or places my kids like to go. At many of my favorite places, I never see another soul, but it's *one* of my favorites. I also don't get the same rush of freedom and what feels like agape I invariably get when I drive into Allagash, and coast into Tyler and Leitha Kelly's place. But I bet it's just like that for other anglers when they drop down the hill in GLS and see the Pine Tree Store, and they know they're about twenty minutes from fishing over wild salmon.

Spring Creeks

Sometimes a pilgrimage turns out to be, well, not so good. Sometimes, it's like when a new girlfriend turns out to have so many issues she becomes less of a girlfriend and more like a project, and the trip becomes more about enlightenment and less about love.

If you live in Maine, are a fly fisher and if you want to fish a spring creek you'd have to drive or fly to upstate New York or to Pennsylvania, right? Not necessarily. Although a real spring creek pilgrimage should probably be to the Beaverkill, or the LeTort (I can hear it now…"What are you saying, my pilgrimage isn't *real?*"), there are, in fact, a few spring creeks in northern Maine.

There are a few in The County (Aroostook…Maine's northern most county): streams with enough limestone and springs to technically qualify as bona fide spring creeks, similar to the ones in Montana and Wyoming—without the elk and the buffalo. Oh, and another big difference...in The County, there is no denied access to water. Anywhere.

If you're a fly rodder, you already know that spring creeks are special to anglers. If you're not sure what the difference is between limestone and freestone streams don't skip this part. Freestone streams (brooks in Maine) are basically water that's run off, tumbling down from mountains or higher elevations. Spring creeks, on the other hand, lie in the bottom of valleys for the most part. (That means that the stream bottoms of limestoners don't get as scoured clean with flooding in the spring, which becomes painfully obvious when you try to wade them.) Spring creeks stay around 50 degrees Fahrenheit, have similar substrates (limestone) and have an abundance of micro invertebrates. Micro invertebrates! Yum. That's when it gets exciting for fly fishers.

Compared to freestone streams, a lot of the insect populations in spring creeks have much longer emergence periods, which translates to longer food availability for the trout. There are often more hatches of mayflies, stoneflies and caddis flies. Basically, the environment in spring creeks is different and therefore, the trout are different. Their coloration is often slightly different and they have a reputation of being a little more selective. I've read that some biologists and fishermen believe that the spring creek trout are more difficult to catch than fish living in freestone streams and rivers. Apparently, because of the long emergence periods of the insects, the spring creek trout become connoisseurs and get a little picky and are harder to fool with feathers and string. Maybe those biologists haven't fished the Henry's Fork of the Snake River in Idaho—a freestone river where all the trout have PhD's in entomology. I'm pretty sure some of those trout can tie their own flies. They see thousands of artificial flies each year. In my experience, all the spring creeks that I've fished are difficult to get to, were relatively easy to fish. Therefore, I'm not so sure about the "high-visibility, a-lot-of-food-on-their-plate-at-all-times"   theories. Sure, if there are tons of insects on the surface while you're trying to entice a trout to choose your artificial, it can seem daunting, but I think most spring creeks are just fished hard...real hard.

To be sure, spring creeks are great. They are treasures and they need to be taken care of. Also, they should be a required pilgrimage for all serious fly rodders.

The most popular limestone stream in The County is Prestile Stream which flows north to south in the eastern part of The County, very close to the border (with Canada, for you New Yorkers, who think Maine *is* in Canada). I wanted to fish the "Stile" as it's called locally (pronounced "Steele") for a long time. Flowing out of a spring-fed reservoir north of the town of

Easton, the stream flows through beautiful farmland, through the towns of Westfield, Mars Hill and Robinson, until it throws a head fake in Bridgewater and then dives east into Canada where it becomes the Presquile River. She originates in a valley, stays in a valley, is spring fed and doesn't flood too much in the springtime, just like the spring creek she's supposed to be. She reportedly has a good insect population, pretty trout and cool water. So my boy and I struck out for the city of Presque Isle, to Aroostook State Park, less than five miles from the stream.

There were two contributing factors to this pilgrimage. Two were favorable, if not downright exciting, and one was obscenely bad. I had been told by several fishermen that Sports Afield (always with the interjection, "at least I think it was Sports Afield") published an article in the early 1950's about the Prestile. It was about how beautiful it was. The stream was crazy-full of brook trout and was listed as "one of the ten best brook trout waters in the world." I can't tell you exactly what it said because I couldn't afford the research fee for the article...especially since it might not have been Sports Afield. Bear in mind that when the article was written, the brook trout fisheries of northern Canada that are famous today, were not really well known in the 1940's and 50's.

Was the Prestile worthy of a pilgrimage? Surely, except the other reading I had done was, to a fisherman, nefarious. Seems in 1960, Freddie Vahlsing, a chubby little rich guy with a penchant for cowboy boots and hat (apparel that would stick out like a sore thumb in The County...which I suppose was the point), basically poisoned the entire Prestile water system—on purpose. Apparently, building and business permits were granted when he applied for and received a license to discharge wastes from a sugar beet refinery in Easton directly into the Prestile. There was already a potato processing plant there. Constraints and requirements were issued along with restrictions and codes to be upheld and, by all accounts, they were all ignored. Like most industrialized things, his potato processing plant produced toxic waste. As the beet refinery neared completion, Vahlsing asked the legislature to downgrade the Prestile from a Class A stream (a classification of a clean, almost drinkable water system) to a Class D...essentially an open sewer, so he could continue to discharge waste directly into the stream. The governor and then Senator Muskie argued on Vahlsing's behalf. The downgrade was permitted (money talks) in spite of protests from locals, farmers, the League of Women Voters, and basically everyone who lived downstream. Within months fish began to die in large numbers.

Reading old reports of the day, it seems like Freddie thought he was bigger than the law. He had lots of friends in Augusta. To save money, he just dumped the waste on the banks of the stream. There are government reports of dead trout floating to the surface by the thousands. A lot of folks who lived near the stream could never get used to the "horrible stench" emitting from the beautiful stream when the water level dropped in the summertime. It got so bad that it created an international incident. For real. In 1968, after a particularly bad fish kill, a group of irate citizens in Centerville, New Brunswick, reached the end of their rope and brought in bulldozers one July morning and dammed up the Prestile at the border. It was largely symbolic, yet real enough...they tore the earthen dam down the next day. I hear there's a monument there, commemorating a "war on pollution." There were a lot more details, but you get the picture. He raped the environment and according to everyone I've spoken to who was there, he couldn't give a crap.

His answer to complaints and allegations was to fly in his private helicopter to the state capital and buy his way out of trouble. Money being what it is it worked on some. He denied charges of inadequate treatment by the Maine Water Improvement Commission. He threw a lot of money at the Maine Democratic Party. He seemed to know a majority of the influential politicians of the day and his lawyer was George Mitchell, who later became the United

States Senate Majority Leader and was the guy who tried to de-steroid baseball. (In Mr. Mitchell's defense, he was a young lawyer at the time and was likely a junior member of a large firm. I don't really know what he personally thought of the Prestile situation.)

Vahlsing eventually went out of business, long after the Prestile was ruined. The story I heard was that he walked by his helicopter one day and one of the rotors chopped off one of his arms. He must not have been paying attention. To karma.

It's important to know that Freddie Vahlsing and state politicians (succumbing to industrialists) did not ruin the Prestile all by themselves. Before the sugar beet refinery was ever built, there was the potato processing plant and residential sewage issues. Starch factory discharges and (talk about the Maine Department of Inland Fisheries and Wildlife dropping the ball) dams were erected with no fish ways, blocking trout migrations. About that...those damned dams. Some were placed to hold back water for irrigation, some for fire protection and some to make pretty little town ponds to skate on. For whatever reason, fish ladders would have been nice. There's historic evidence of an Atlantic salmon run in the Prestile before all the impoundments were placed. In 1973, the main obstruction in Tracey Mills, New Brunswick, was breeched by high spring flows and Atlantic salmon were there again as far upstream as the dam in Robinson, Maine. In 1970, the dam at Robinson washed out and rebuilt by the town three years later, when it was, the local anglers wanted a fishway installed and there was quite brouhaha. The MDIFW recommended the town not include a fishway in an effort to manage the upper Prestile for a brook trout fishery. The idea was that the young salmon might compete with the existing brook trout population. They might've been right, but there are locals who are still pissed about that to this day. I suppose the state also considered that the Canadians could rebuild the Tracey Mills dam at any time, for whatever reason, and that would put an end to the salmon run anyway.

When reading about the Prestile and listening to stories from middle-aged men who fished the stream with their fathers and grandfathers, it's sickening to think of the disregard to a once famous trout stream. A friggin' *limestone* stream, no less!

It had been raining pretty hard when we made our way to the 'Stile on the forty-second anniversary (to the day) of the Canadian "dam protest" in Centerville. But the skies cleared while we rigged our rods and the temperature rose. It was mid-morning and I smelled a Blue Winged Olive hatch. The stream didn't look much different than most streams in Maine, pretty, as it slid through a cedar forest, dark and cool with tall ferns choking both banks. Prior to the recent rains it had been a dry spring and the stream, maybe forty-feet wide in some spots, was quite shallow. As we rigged our rods, it became apparent that we were next to an ATV trail. Six or seven machines went ripping through the stream, each one straining under the load of at least one 300-pound person. So much for not scaring the fish.

The stream looked healthy from the bank, but once we started wading it was pretty hard to ignore the "structure." Here and there, where the ATV trail cut through the water, was an I-beam emerging from the muddy bottom, an old clothes dryer, a cigarette pack and an orange Croc shoe—a left, size seven. Fifty yards downstream it got better.

I checked the bushes along the banks and found some tan, size 16 caddis flies fluttering around. There were a few nymphs under some rocks I overturned. I didn't turn the I-beam over.

I tied on an elk-hair caddis and my son went with his go to searching pattern, a small Royal Wulff. We fished steady for a couple of hours and caught only one six-inch brookie. As I said earlier, limestone streams don't get as flushed with spring flooding and man, the going was tough. The stream bottom was strewn with logs, branches and boulders. More than any other streams or brooks I wade.

We called it a day and went back to the campsite. There are two contradictory things that are great parts of fishing trips: the peaceful solitude and meeting and talking to interesting people. While the two can't collide, they often occur on the same trip. It happened on this one. Scott Thompson and Jim Nadeau, two of the park rangers at Aroostook State Park, are fly fishers. They made some time for us and we talked for a long time about their personal histories with the Prestile, the Vahlsing days and what the stream means to them today. There aren't as many fly fishers as in southern Maine, or at least it seems to be the case. It could be that fly fishers in The County just don't talk about it as much, or dress in LL Bean breathable waterproof wading jackets— wool still works. It's farm country, and as the Man said, "form ever follows function."

Scott Thompson's grandfather, Walter Thompson, was one of the old timey, well-known fly rodders in the storied days when the 'Stile was famous. He also was one of the few commercial fly tiers in the north country. He was the innovator of several streamers and tied the Thompson Special, a dry fly tied specifically for the Prestile and nearby Presque Isle streams. The Special was a kind of Royal Wulff-Hendrickson-Coachman, forward-wing hybrid, tied rather sparsely. Unbelievably, Scott gifted me one of the last Thompson Specials Walter tied, shortly before he died while in his nineties. I suppose it's possible that Walter tied thousands of these and they're just in the grandchildren's way. But more likely, Scott has a few left, cherishes them, and perhaps realized my passion for the sport and gave me the fly knowing that it will mean something. It does.

We talked about Scott's memories of fishing with his grandfather, about the fish, the hatches and the artificials. We talked about the botched dam (no fish ladder), in Mars Hill, and we talked about one of Scott's major concerns...agricultural runoff. I hit the hay counting down the strikes the Prestile has against it. For instance, how it flows right through several towns and has easy access for a lot of local meat fishermen who kill their limit of legal fish, every time they can.

The next morning we tried the stream again, a little farther downstream, in a section Scott often fished with his elders. While rigging up, I wished I could try the old Thompson Special, but knew I could not. My son tied on old reliable, one of his Royal Wulffs, while I tried a #18 Adams. The water had cleared quite a bit and the temperature was 54 degrees. I saw a few small tan-colored mayflies but couldn't catch one. They looked like size 18 Blue Winged Olives but I couldn't be sure. I shook some bushes, turned over some rocks and sat and watched for a while but didn't see much else. We started fishing, working our way downstream...not my favorite direction, but it didn't matter too much. This was a pilgrimage, after all. Catching fish becomes almost secondary.

I could imagine this pretty little stream being at one time a first rate trout fishery, so far from any urban population. I've never seen a photo of Walter Thompson, but it wasn't hard to imagine him through the alders and poplars, carefully wading along the edge of the stream making perfect roll casts to the heads of the pools with his old fiberglass fly rod...or maybe he used one of those wispy old Shakespeare split-cane rods (which maybe were alright for nymphing, but sucked for roll casts). He probably kept his elbow tucked and his wrist straight. I'll bet he wore a short-brimmed hat and smoked a pipe. I don't know. I have an affinity for those men and women in the old days, especially the not-so-rich ones who fly fished—*only* fly fished. Other fishermen would raise their eyebrows at the slow-casting, methodical anglers because they were a bit different. They were passionate and they were interesting.

Neither my son nor I could get a fish to rise and eat a fly. There wasn't any activity on the water's surface and there was no real hatch going on. I remember thinking if we got skunked, it would put us in pretty good company. A lot of people—good fly fishers—have come up empty on spring creeks. As I said, the 'Stile, technically, is a limestone stream.

After an hour of being fishless, my mind started to wander (it does that a lot).

It seemed no part of the stream was very far from tilled farm fields. Often you could see bits of farm fields through the trees, but when you couldn't, you could sense they were there. From all the fields there were tiny rivulets, still wet from the previous day's rains. On the outside edge of a bend pool, lying in the mud, a dead fish caught my eye. About three inches long, the parr marks were unmistakable...it was a brook trout—a fry, actually. My boy and I talked about it a bit, and wondered why it died. Two more steps downstream and another dead fish caught my eye. I stood there for a moment and, looking around, saw another...and another. There were many. I took some photos and sat on the bank thinking about Scott's concerns about agricultural runoff. I'm no scientist and can't say exactly what killed those small trout, but rain runoff from the crop fields makes the most sense to me. Certainly the smallest, youngest members in most species are more susceptible to all manner of toxins, chemical ingestions, and even environmental extremes like depleted oxygen levels.

I'm glad Scott wasn't there to see his stream, with its muddy edges littered with either poisoned or suffocated little trout. I'm especially glad his grandfather didn't see it. It was pretty disturbing. My son was fifteen at the time. And even he seemed to understand the ridiculousness of squandering such a beautiful resource.

In the end, I caught a couple small brookies on a hare's ear nymph. We took a little time to think things over, and I left there wondering what could be done to restore the stream. I can empathize with the farmers along the stream...I used to be a farmer and I know how tough it can be. I still have a state pesticide license for God's sake. But it appears the biggest threat to the 'Stile these days are nutrient runoff from farms and erosion. I'll bet most of the farmers are working with state officials in any way they can. There must be some solution, somewhere. Otherwise, we'll have to ask ourselves, what are we consuming, potatoes, or world-class fisheries? We've already consumed the Prestile's history. Hopefully we can be better stewards of its future. In spite of all the Prestile has been through, it has never stopped trying to hang in there. The brookies also haven't stopped trying...and neither should we.

No Quarry for a Gentleman

Bradley, Maine August 2010

Mainers have a love/hate relationship with bass. While we like being known as a trout and salmon (gamefish) state, we also happen to have a world-class smallmouth bass fishery. Most Mainers I've met simply prefer brook trout. That said, a lot of the fly fishers I know will, on occasion, fish for bass. Don't get me wrong...we really do love the gamefish (sometimes we love 'em to death). Maine holds the largest population of landlocked salmon and native brook trout in the United States, but some of us cannot live on salmonids and charr alone.

In the 1960's and '70's when I was a kid, no one I knew fished for bass. If someone caught one they were disgusted and might even throw the fish into the woods. Those that did occasionally fish for bass or pickerel were a small minority.

Times do change. While a lot of Mainers still feel the same about bass, in late summer when many of the hatches peeter off, or on those days when there isn't enough time to drive the hour or two to one of the more famous tailwaters that are scattered throughout the state, friends and I will strike out for smallies. Smallies are the one species I will sometimes purposely fish off of their spawning beds, always releasing them, but I haven't for years. Every winter my fly fishing buddies will say, "This year we're fishing the River (the Penobscot) in June during the spawn." But when June arrives we can't seem to sacrifice a prime caddis or mayfly hatch to cast for the males guarding their beds, even though it's amazing fun...floating downstream, casting poppers carelessly under over-hanging branches, next to boulders or near downed trees.

The male bass takes care of the spawning. He alone builds and cares for the nest. When the water temperature is in the mid-fifties, he selects a bed of gravel in water anywhere from ten inches to twelve feet deep. Using his tail as a whisk broom, he starts up "uphill" in the water and clears out a circular area about two times his length and when finished, he sits and waits for the female to arrive when she's damned good and ready. When she has made him wait long enough (once the water warms up a few more degrees), she shows up and lays her eggs. When I was quite young, I was occasionally invited to spend weekends at a boyhood chum's camp on Branch Pond in Ellsworth. I vividly remember one morning laying on a flat rock that jutted out into the lake over about three feet of water. I could clearly see a small bass patrolling his nest. If you've never been to Branch Pond, the water is gin clear. It was so clear I could see his eyes, and the way he curled his tail, even when he was sitting still. I was the only camper up that early and was mesmerized by the scene. After about forty-five minutes, the young male didn't seem to mind my presence. I experimented by putting my hand and arm in the water. It wasn't long before I gained his confidence and he allowed the intrusion. After a while, I pulled my hand from the lake and moved onto daydreaming, undoubtedly about distant lands, or girls. At one point, the little male darted from the nest toward the deeper lake and I lost sight of him. He returned a few moments later with another, slightly larger bass. I couldn't tell if they were fighting or playing, but after a while—I swear to God—they laid side-by-side. I couldn't actually see any eggs, but it was apparent that the first sex I ever saw was fish sex. I wonder if perhaps that is why I love trout so much.

Once the deed is done, the nest-guarding male becomes very aggressive. That's when it's so much fun to fish top-water plugs. Fishermen, by our actions, definitely elicit an attack. A six-inch smallmouth's diet is comprised of 80% fish with the remainder insects, leaches and especially, crayfish. So when we throw a top-water fly over a spawning bed it's antagonistic. The only way to fish a popper during the spawn is *slowly*. If you retrieve it too quickly, the bass may feel there's no real threat to the eggs. Let the fly sit good and long, and then give it the slightest strip of line. The smallest ripple on the water made by the fly the better, and be ready when the cartwheeling bass explodes into the air. It never gets old. As I said, we always release them, and if it stresses them a lot...they're just bass, right? I fish some states where it's legal to fish for trout during their spawn, but I won't do it. It just doesn't seem right.

There are some rules for the trout fly fisherman when "Bassin." We NEVER get upset if we break off a huge bass. Instead, we just laugh (or snicker) and say, rather matter-of-factly, "...that was a heavy fish, actually." We never stand there and admire the fish...or kiss them, or release them gently, or resuscitate them. We toss them back into the water from whatever height we happen to be. Sometimes we'll say things like "These things are pigs!" But we'll never use the words "Hawg" or "pretty" or "beautiful" when we catch one. "Nice" is a possibility. More often you might hear one of us say, "Jesus...the fly is bigger than the fish!" We pretend that our flyfishing for them somehow honors them. It's as if we're saying, "Hey...Bass...we're trout guys, but we're here. There are no trout, you're here, we'll just catch you, taunt you a little and toss you back...how'd that be? You'll be better for it." The hypocrisy of fishermen can be boundless.

Personally, I just like catching fish with a fly and a rod—preferably with a cane rod. If I don't catch anything, I'm happy just fishing. I've been known to stand for hours in one spot, delightfully catching chubs by the dozens, or even sunfish. (Smallmouth bass are sunfish, by the way.) I love it. If I can shuffle on down the stream and catch trout, of course I'll do that. But if there is little chance of gamefish for whatever reason (no hatches, the time of day, they don't exist there...), then I'm fine with the "trash fish."

Take bluegills for instance. I bet if you caught an eight-inch bluegill on a 2-weight fly rod, and then caught a brook trout of equal length the fight would go to the bluegill. I remember hearing Lefty Kreh once say if you tied a smallmouth and a brook trout of equal size tail-to-tail, the bass would tow the trout around all day long. That's probably true, but the trout would have an annoyed, smug look on its face and the bass would just go on swimming in circles, wondering why the going got tough.

While the West Branch of the Penobscot River is all about salmon and huge brook trout, the river's East Branch and the main river below the town of Millinocket, are regarded as having one of the best smallmouth fisheries in the Northeastern United

States. Some of the serious bass anglers in Maine might disagree with that stature. I must say some of the best bass fishing I've had was Downeast, in the vicinity of Grand Lake Stream. I don't know...I live along the banks of the lower Penobscot north of Bangor. So the few times each year I fish for bass, it's within five minutes of the house. Walking. Grand Lake Stream is one of those neat old communities in the Maine woods where the hunting, fishing and guiding tradition is folded into the fabric of the town and the people. You can't read any literature about the place without seeing an old photograph of Ted Williams (*the* Ted Williams) holding up a string of nice, dead smallies, caught on a fly, presumably. My man Curt Gowdy fished there a lot also.

Although I've had the pleasure of fly fishing for bass in places like Virginia, Texas and Florida, one of my favorite bassin' memories (I'm excluding the Peacock bass in Venezuela and Panama), is fishing the mouth of Grand Lake Stream where it flows into Big Lake near the township of Princeton. One memorable day in April just after ice-out, taking a break from the usual method at that time of year of trolling flies just below the surface for salmon, we were trying to locate salmon to cast to them. It rarely works for me, but it's fun anyway. My Florida friend John Jasztrebski and I anchored my 1937 Rangely guide boat in the cove at the mouth of the stream when he made a long cast up into the stream proper and hooked a nice fish on a Nine-Three streamer. When he got it close enough to the boat to see what it was, we could see it was a bass...a *big* bass. When John hoisted it into the boat, it vomited a whole bunch of big, black stone fly nymphs—size eight, I think. Usually when I see something or someone throw up, a gag response in my own gullet rears its ugly head, but not then. It was early in the season and I had been dreaming all winter about casting a fly, retrieving it and hooking a fish...*any* fish. Here was a chance.

We scrambled to find the size-eight black stones in the fly boxes and started casting.

We were anchored behind them and kept casting over their backs with a little weight and no indicator. The nymphs didn't sink more than a couple of feet when the chartreuse end of the fly line would dart up stream. We stood in the boat and caught at least a dozen bass. Here's the kicker...I doubt any of them were less than four pounds. In Maine, good-sized, mature smallies average two-to-three pounds with four plus pounders being landed occasionally. The state record smallmouth is eight pounds. In other words, they were nice fish, all of 'em.

As I said, that was the kicker, now here's the point. A couple of salmon-fishing, fly-rodding trout nuts had an amazing day of fishing—a day still remembered—catching bass. We caught a few salmon earlier that day, but it is those bass I remember in detail.

Bass were introduced in Maine in 1869. I guess that turned out alright...it's hard to imagine we had to do anything to "improve" an already world-class, cold water fishery. On the other hand, we had built so many mills and dams in Maine by then that perhaps someone in state government felt they needed to do something with all that backed-up, warm water. My father and his father before him were railroad men. My grandfather worked for the Boston and Maine in the 1800's. My Dad told me stories of how stocking fish in the early days was often done by the firemen and brakemen on the trains. Sent along their routes with buckets of fish, they would make unscheduled stops and dump the buckets into brooks and streams designated by the "government men." I believe the stories. In those days there were no fisheries commissioners and fishery biology was unknown. Most of the early "stockers" were adamant that bass weren't stocked into any salmonid or trout waters, but over the past 100 years bass and other non-native fish species have been illegally introduced into well over 100 bodies of water in Maine. There were so many good fishing lakes in Maine, nobody worried about the salmon and trout populations. They should have. The bass absolutely do effect coldwater species.

They predate the juvenile salmon and trout, as well as the forage fish populations. As usual, once the hardy bass drove out the more selective trout, Man blamed their mistakes on the bass.

There are very few ponds in Maine where there is absolutely no chance, ever, of flooding in the spring and therefore contaminating adjacent or contiguous waters. And I don't know of many without an outlet. Only a moron would chance introducing non-native species into any pond that could potentially contaminate a complete watershed. To fly fishers, the so-called "bucket biologists" (much too kind a title) are akin to the worst criminals in society. Many years ago I helped with stocking a small alpine spring pond with a non-native species. Even though it was with official permission and on private property, I only agreed after extensively hiking around the spring-fed pond and was satisfied there was no place the fish could go (it had no inlet nor outlet), no matter if there was a flood (impossible) or if the fish evolved and sprouted legs (almost impossible). While it was in no way like an illegal stocking of non-native fish into a river system in Maine, it still felt funny. I have since known many small, private ponds in Maine that are stocked with brook trout from time to time. I'm cool with it, as long as they're trout.

The whole "trash fish" vs. gamefish thing gets a little difficult to swallow sometimes.

I get it, but it seems a dight unfair. I've heard the bass-against-traditional, coldwater species described as a culture war. That sounds a little harsh, but the trout-and-salmon proponents and the biologists charged with managing the state's fisheries (a daunting task), are increasingly becoming defensive. I took a family friend, who happens to be a bass fisherman from Massachusetts, for a lazy afternoon fishing at Pleasent River Lake (one of my "home waters"). The lake used to be a decent salmon lake in the 1960's and 70's and is now managed for splake. Smallmouths were illegally introduced there around 1980, and there are notices placed around the lake by the Maine Department of Inland Fish and Wildlife asking anglers to kill all bass caught there in an effort to keep the population down. When my friend, I'll call him Ed Boulay (because that's his name), caught a nice smallie over three pounds, there was quite a brouhaha over its impending death. Culture clash. Some folks think a perfect day of fishing is in a bass boat on a bass lake with plenty of refreshments on-board. Others might think it's a six-mile hike into the back-country to a remote pond to catch a hexagenia hatch at sunset, with only a water filter to stave-off certain death from dehydration.

Mainers appreciate our traditions. Observers "from away" often mistakenly describe our lack of enthusiasm regarding federal agencies micro managing our wildlife departments as "backwards" (sometimes keeping the Feds at bay is a good tack). In contrast, we citizen observers and sportsmen simply see the efforts and ability to learn and adjust by our fisheries managers as, quite frankly, doing a better job than many of the states where the Feds come from. Somehow, Maine's Department of Inland Fisheries and Wildlife has managed to stare development and illegal introductions in the face and maintain, protect and even grow our fragile, native fish species. To keep from getting too pissed off, most fly fishers I know just keep telling themselves that criminals who toss buckets of bass into our river systems "know not what they do." Truth is, they probably do know...they just don't care about tradition, the native fish, or the tireless work of fisheries professionals, or anything, it seems, but themselves.

Alright, alright...enough about that. The bottom line for me and for most of my fly fishing buddies is that we prefer gamefish and want to hang on to our traditional, storied trout and salmon waters. But we like and appreciate the bass, bluegill and sunfish. And for the very select few of us, even the chub. That's as hard to write as it is to say. Chubs in Maine are actually fallfish. For years I've said that if a Dad or a Mom wants to teach a youngster how to cast a fly, present it on the water, set a hook and play a fish, they should find a little hole somewhere chock full of chubs. Sunnies work nearly as well.

It's interesting to note that most Mainers don't seem to know what to think of white perch. They're not a "gamefish" species, but we love 'em. I know families that will drive for many miles to a pond or a lake that holds white perch. They're one of the sweetest tasting fish, and I caught one through the ice at Mopang Lake once that weighed two pounds. It was so big I wasn't even positive it was a perch. My mother always made fish chowder from them. Most people now catch a pail of them and then filet them for a fish fry. They are a schooling fish and are easily caught once they're found. When we were kids we would catch them by the boat load, just before (and after) dark. Once the frenzy started they could be caught on a bare hook. Nowadays, they are more fun to catch on a size 16 Parachute Adams with a three-weight fly rod, as are all fish.

Hard Water

Bradley, January, 2010

Our kids are young, and once the water gets hard enough, we go ice fishing. It's a long way from fly fishing, obviously, but it's still fishing.

While I will fly fish when I'm sore, hungry, bleeding, cold, hot, with hooks stuck in my flesh, and in all manner of weather, I'm pretty wimpy on the ice. The forecast has to be at least in the twenties, not too windy, and it needs to be sunny with at least six or eight inches of ice. I'm 230 pounds and have size nine feet. I'm built for breaking through.

We typically don't go to the big, famous salmon lakes where there are tons of people and dozens of ATV's and snowmobiles going 400 miles-per-hour. We walk, pulling sleds with traps, bait, extra clothes, lunch, and we drill the holes with a small hand auger. Managing the hand auger is a little tough with a rotator cuff worn thin from years of abuse, but you'd be surprised how often guys will swing by with a Jiffy power auger and offer free services to drill a few holes. I usually get the feeling that the benevolent chums feel sorry for me, but I don't care...I take them up on it. Truth is, they don't feel sorry for me...invariably they're just being nice. Some local Maine ice fishermen might read this and be disgusted that I'm such a fair-weather (meaning wimpy...or *spleeny*) ice fisherman, but I can't help it

Sometimes you can learn a few things ice fishing which can be helpful when the open-water season finally comes around. More than once I've gone to some remote pond to put up a few traps in the ice, drilled a couple of holes and turned the slush surrounding the holes black with stonefly nymphs. One pond in particular holds some three to four pound native brookies. I'd had a hard time figuring out the water (a fly fisher's way of saying he or she has been skunked, over and over) and had never tried big, black, #10 stonefly nymphs. It's not like I'd unlocked a mystery, but I did have some ammunition for the next spring.

Last weekend was another good example of how ice fishing can be helpful. We loaded-up the kids and struck out for a local pond, less than an hour from home, which we like and have fished before, in summer and winter. Fifteen to twenty years ago when we last fished it, there was a good population of pickerel, smallmouth bass, yellow perch, the occasional landlocked salmon, and brown trout. My wife wanted to go there instead of somewhere closer because of the likelihood of the kids getting a lot of flags. (That's what mothers do...consider the kids first.) I'd heard there were no longer many brown trout in there and certainly, no more salmon, but the perch would keep the kids busy. And they did. I don't think I stopped baiting hooks and setting traps while everyone else ran from flag to flag for the first hour. It didn't take long for the kids to start hauling out nice, fat browns—fourteen inches, then fifteen, then about eighteen inches...nice! One of the nearby benevolent, hole-drilling guys came over when they heard my son yell "Hey Dad! It's a trout!" They said they hadn't seen a trout come out of there for an "awfully long time."

I told the kids we could mark the spot by laying two sticks on the ice and making an "X." We'd come back to that spot and fish it in the spring. They didn't buy it.

We marked the spot, on the Gazetteer, and thought about how we would fly fish there in the spring. We headed home when the wind picked up. We only had one shiner left in the bait bucket anyway. My wife made the short walk back to the Jeep with some of the gear while our son and our ten-year-old daughter helped pick up the traps and packed the sled. My daughter Sam was in charge of emptying the bait bucket and policing the area, like picking up any water and soda bottles that might not have made it into the recycle bag. Before we even got back to the Jeep, my son noticed his sister carrying a soda bottle with water in it. She was guarding it pretty carefully and a closer look revealed the last little shiner swimming around in it, promoted from bait to pet in an instant. She named it "Chubs." People say she might be a Vet when she grows up.

Ice fishing in Maine is fairly popular, I'd say, but nowhere near as it is with crazy people from places like Wisconsin (the Maine of the west). I've seen people there with ice shacks that were nicer than our house, with wall-to-wall carpeting, propane heat and solar power backup. I saw one guy out there with a satellite dish set up on his shack's roof—probably so's he could watch the Packers. That's probably the kind of ice shack God would have if He could afford it. It's pretty cool, actually, and although in warmer months I'm a bit of a fly fishing purist, I think anything that helps get you through the winter is a good thing, providing it's legal, of course. Only problem is, I think that most of what they fish for in that part of the country is walleye. I'm sure they're good eating. But if we had them in Maine, we would probably lump them into the "trash fish" category which chubs, suckers, bass, yellow perch, and pickerel fall into—especially yellow perch. Most Mainers I know simply throw them out onto the ice for the bald eagles to pick up. I don't know one Mainer that would attempt eating one. The species that are not on the trash fish list are; salmon (both Atlantic and Landlocked), whitefish, splake, and any kind of trout...brook trout being the favorite of most locals.

I won't go into the techniques or favorite tricks of ice fishing. Partly because it would probably be boring, but mostly because I don't know them. For me it all comes down to which species of forage fish to choose (depends on what you're fishing for and where your fishing), where to impale the bait with the hook (through the mouth or behind the dorsal fin) and how deep to lower the bait. I never know. So in some of the holes, I put the hook in the mouth and in other holes the alternative. In some ice holes, the bait goes near bottom, some just under the ice and some in the middle. Problem is, when we start getting flags, I can never remember which hole is which. Not very empirical. There seems to be a movement these days to use bright red hooks instead of the old normal ones. I don't know...I use both, but I never remember which ones I catch fish with.

Another benefit of ice fishing is that game fish are cruising around during winter months taking food when they find it. While fly fishing requires skill and knowledge acquired over time, anyone with an ice trap can luck into some pretty big fish from time to time. Recently someone pulled a brook trout over nine pounds through the ice in Mousam Lake. There was a photo of it in the Bangor Daily News, of course. It's a new state record. (Although it was a stocked fish.) I saw the photo and was a little sad. I do kill a few brookies from time to time—but that fish, stocked or not, should have been caught in a river on a streamer fly, with a 5 weight rod, after a tough battle, and in fast, heavy water, then released to die from old age, holding court over the lesser fish in the river. I've had biologists tell me that if I'm going to harvest trout, go for a "slot" size. There's no such law in Maine, but keeping a few small fish or the very big, old pigs that will probably not reproduce again, makes sense. Throw back the nice, big, gene-pool enhancing fish, with years of reproduction in them. But a nine-pound brookie?! Jeezum! If that fellow snapped a photo and then shoved that big 'ole trout back under the ice he could have talked about it forever. He could have put a big photo up at the local bar and he would always have the memory. A *great* memory.

As I write this, a week after our last ice fishing outing, it occurs to me that Chubs is still swimming in an old fish bowl over the kitchen sink. Somehow Sam has kept him alive. You can count on fishing to build memories, even if it's a half-dead chub in a fish bowl.

Fly Box

I've got friends who are definitely fly junkies and some who are, for various reasons, fly minimalists. The junkies seem driven to have every variation of every fly pattern known to the western world (and some from abroad) in their boxes; the minimalists, obviously, not so much. My boy is a minimalist. I think he'd be happy enough with assorted sizes of four flies: Royal Wulffs, Whooly Buggers, Pheasant Tail Nymphs and Stimulators. If I had to pick only four for myself, I guess I would substitute the Wulffs for Elk Hair Caddis. But I *don't* have to pick just four, and although I don't carry hundreds of flies, I'd categorize myself as a "fly pragmatist", not a junkie and not a minimalist. I try really hard to stock my boxes with nothing more than what I'm quite sure will be necessary in the area (or region) I'll be fishing. It's way too easy to go overboard.

There's no iron-clad rule to follow when choosing the correct fly. We all have our favorite flies we love to fish and are the most comfortable with. In Northern

New England, where I now live, there are some great caddis hatches all summer, so I have a lot of sizes and variations of Elk Hair Caddis dries and pupal patterns. If nothing is happening in the air or on the water's surface but I'm driven to fish dries, I'll start with a small Elk Hair dry or a small Stimulator...especially as we get later in the season. Since trout consume about 90% of their food underwater, (the percentage changes, depending upon who you talk to) 90% of the time I start with a fly like a soft hackle partridge, pheasant tail nymph or a caddis pupa. If nothing takes, I'll try a leech pattern. Trout *love* leeches...it's like an injection of pure protein for the trout.

I don't fish streamers nearly as much as most fly fishers. It's well known that swinging a streamer will sometimes illicit a response from bigger fish, but since I've gotten older I don't feel driven to catch huge trout, and because I like nymphing and dry fly fishing, I usually just stick with those. There are times when streamers are the only way to go, so I carry a complement of patterns that work well in Maine. Some are favorites and some are simply patterns that have been popular in certain waters for generations. For fresh water, I usually carry Joe's Smelts, Nine-Three's, Montreal Whores, Pink Ladys, Grey and Black Ghosts, Muddler Minnows, Barn's Specials, Deadly Dauph (not my invention, but I like the name) and one or two Mickey Finns. All of my friends carry Hornbergs, and they're a productive fly, but I've never liked them and I don't know why. Whooly Buggers are technically streamers, but I put them in a class of their own. I always have four times as many Buggers as all the rest of the bait fish-type streamers. You can see that's not a lot of streamer flies.

Dry flies are another matter. The "dry box," when full, will have (in two or three sizes of each) Blue Wing Olives, Irresistibles, Black Gnats, Adams, Little Yellow Stones, Stimulators, CDC Comparaduns, Elk Hair Caddis, Sulfur Duns, March Browns, Light Hendricksons, Red Quills, Red and Green Humpys, Royal Wulffs, a few Parachute Spinners (A.K. Best's), Brown and Green Drakes, and some CDC Biot Spinners. I'm such a believer in presentation that I swear if you carry those dries in Maine, that's all you'll need to catch any fish that might be looking up.

Terrestrials are a separate category, but I keep them in the dry fly box. I like to have three or more variations of ants. I've seen some hellacious flying ant hatches in the Allagash. I like a simple black foam beetle with a little parachute on top and some orange on the underside of the abdomen. In most of Maine the orange is *very* important. A few green and a few orange grasshoppers usually top off my terrestrials (I'm not including the bass bug terrestrials here).

The nymph box has a heart, soul and mind of its own. Once you get the feel for nymph fishing, it can be the most productive method of fresh water fishing there is. I once read a passage in a book that basically said a good nymph fisherman could effectively "fish-out" a trout stream in a lifetime of fishing. I *think* I read that. It could have been said "upta" fishing camp back when I was drinking. Wherever it came from, the statement carries the same weight.

I usually carry two small nymph boxes. They're not the most organized things...especially once the season gets going and I'm fishing hard. They're pretty though, when I start organizing them around the beginning of March. The flies are usually stuck in the boxes, the smallest at the top, with the largest stoneflies and drakes at the bottom. I put all the flashbacks together, and then the pheasant tails, the caddis pupas, scuds and chironomids are grouped together. One box, when full, might have 200-300 nymphs in it. But I go through a lot in a season. If you're not getting fetched on bottom from time to time (and losing flies) then you're probably not getting down deep enough. If you are just getting into nymph fishing and live in Maine, then you might want to start out with a few bead-head pheasant tails, some green caddis pupa (with dark heads) and a few small bead-head soft hackle partridge flies. The soft hackles are best fished just under the surface, or in the surface film. Sometimes they're fished dead-drift, and at times we'll "skitter" them quickly on the surface.

I keep all the saltwater stuff in a separate little backpack. The reels, spools, leaders, tippet, flies, clippers, hemostats and sinking headers are all in there, that way if I'm in route somewhere and I see stripers or even mackerel close to shore, I can quickly grab the 8-weight and the salt bag and I'm ready. I don't take the fly vest.

At this point you're probably thinking, why is this guy telling me how he arranges his fly boxes? Well, if you're a beginner, you might want a bit of guidance about such matters. If you're an experienced fly fisher, you might glean something regarding local flies (at least one opinion).

If you're a Mainer and you already know what flies work in Maine, I'm still covered. The winters are so long and brutal, that I know come January you'll read just about anything about fly fishing, even an essay about some other guy's fly boxes.

Bass bugs. They're fun. I have two big boxes (which I also keep separated from my "game fish" gear) filled with all manner of gaudy flies. There's no rhyme nor reason to the boxes...they're just stuffed willy-nilly with deer hair mice, various poppers, swimming frogs, some over-sized foam ants and beetles, and some *huge* Chernobyl ants. The poppers are always fun to fish, but I discovered something interesting a couple of seasons ago. I never really considered using Chernobyl ants in Maine, but I actually believe that bass, when they're on their spawning beds and see a big Chernobyl they feel threatened by it. If you have the patience to let it sit (with some barely perceptible movement) anywhere near a bed, the bass will attack it with particular attitude. And pickerel will turn themselves inside-out to get at them. No sipping...I'm just saying. I don't know exactly what Maine insect the Chernobyl mimics that make the bass feel so threatened, but I tried it on several lakes and ponds vs. other flies, and the results were so consistent that I now use a Chernobyl as a starter fly during the bass spawn.

I do have one special fly box that I keep a little more organized than the others. In fact, I make a real effort to keep it full and stocked appropriately after every outing. It's the "small stream box" and it's labeled just that with indelible ink on the front. A few times a week during the season, I stop and try one of the many small brooks I pass on the way home from somewhere. In it I keep a full complement of flies to cover most situations I might encounter on a brook or stream. It allows me to simplify. Rather than rigging up all my gear and carrying a lot of stuff, I can shove the box in a pocket, grab some tippet material and a pair of snippers and be off. It's liberating to shed my old vest once in a while, especially now that the vest is so full of gear. It doesn't feel well balanced without the landing net hanging off the magnet in the back.

I believe more thought goes into what goes into my "small stream box" than occurs at my annual physical. The box is only about 5" x 3-3/4", so economy of flies is key. I've established that I'm not the biggest streamer fisherman, so I stick in one row of small (#10) Gray Ghost, Nine-Three's and about six Whooly Buggers...three black (with red heads...I like the redheads) and three olive. Terrestrials go in next, directly under the row of streamers. A few Grasshoppers, some Flying Ants, and a couple of Fat-Head Foam beetles are usually enough. Then come the dries; three rows of different sized Hendricksons, Red Quills, half a row of Green Drakes, a few Black Gnats, some Blue Wing Olives, at least six Stimulators, a whole row of Elk Hair Caddis, a few Wulffs and some CDC spinners. That will fill up one side of the box.

The other side is devoted to nymphs, pupas, chironomids and soft hackles. As I get older I'm becoming more of a believer in soft hackle flies, so there are quite a few of them in there. I tie a simple partridge soft hackle in green, orange and some in a dark red body. Belfast, Maine, fly-tyer Moe DeCoteau, ties the best soft hackle I've seen. I'd like to buy them from him regularly, but he might be the most generous guy on the planet, and he probably would try to give them away...I wish he sold flies. I'm hoping he'll start selling them as he closes in on retirement. Truth be told, that small stream box would likely be just fine for ninety percent of the fishing I do. The idea of becoming a minimalist is always appealing, but I can't seem to do anything minimally.

You shouldn't put all your eggs, or flies, in one basket. A few years ago I dropped a box with perhaps 200 flies into the Aroostook River. It was hard to watch it float away, but going after it would have been death defying. If that had been all of my dries, or nymphs, or streamers I had with me it would have been disastrous. The small stream box saved me on that day. In fact it's probably smart to have at least a small mixture of flies in each box.

I hope someone found that lost fly box up in The County. I especially hope it was a youngster, desperately in need of dozens of Hendricksons. And as if losing the fly box wasn't enough, I seem to recall I was skunked that day also. Awesome.

The Greying of a Fly Fisher

MDI, Maine 2011

I remember quite well the first time I realized I was getting old. I was twenty-six. It was on a football field in Vancouver, BC and the issue was an A/C separation in the left shoulder. Surely I had been the happy recipient of a lot of injuries by then...torn ligaments, stretched tendons and broken bones that required surgeries, but that shoulder separation, that tearing-away of the acromioclavicular joint really, really hurt. It wasn't the initial pain from the injury, I could play through that, it was the ominous feeling, the *knowing* that this was going to take a long time to come back from. And it did. Until that day I hadn't worried too much about the injuries and figured they were just part of the game. In those days, I didn't worry about much at all. The only physical issues that concerned me were "how fast, how strong and how fit." I had a six-pack then. These days I have a family pack. O.K., I'll admit it...it's a pony keg.

A generation later, the left shoulder rarely bothers me at all...it's the right that aches from time to time, on account of a rotator cuff worn a little thin from at least (and this is a reasonable estimate) 1,404,000 casts. Sounds like a lot, but it's not. The mechanism that seems to aggravate a rotator cuff the most is abduction (lifting your elbow straight out to the side) and overhead stuff. So a rotator cuff definitely comes into play in fly fishing. I know what you're thinking...when casting a fly one shouldn't have one's hand overhead. But you don't know me, and I spend a *lot* of time reaching into trees. For flies, you see.

I'll bet you're also thinking, "What the hell is a rotator cuff, anyway?" While many of the joints in the human body aren't that complex, the shoulder is unique. The knee, for example is a "sliding hinge" joint, the hip, a "ball & socket" but the shoulder is more like a universal joint (though not completely). Most all of the joints are held in place or, constrained, by a number of soft tissues. The ligaments are the obvious structures. For instance, the knee is not a complicated joint, but it needs all of its parts to work correctly. The leg bends at the knee, the femur slides and rotates. The anterior and posterior cruciate ligaments keep the femur from sliding too far forward and backward. The medial and lateral collateral ligaments aid in side-to-side stability. Then there's the joint capsule, the retinaculum, the musculature of the quads and the hamstrings, and the medial and lateral meniscus (which most folks think of as a "cushion" or shock absorber) functioning in concert for a stable knee and a normal gait. So you see, even in a relatively simple joint there's a lot of crap going on in there.

The shoulder, at least to me, is a bit more complicated. There are many contributing structures that constrain the joint while allowing the proper range of motion, but here's the basics of the rotator cuff. (Now hang in there.) It's a combination of four muscles and a few tendons that form a covering over the very top of the upper arm bone (humerus). The cuff has two main functions. It holds the head of the humerus in place in the joint and enables the arm to rotate. When part of it tears, there's usually weakness in the arm and pain when lifting it, or when lowering it from a raised position. A tear can be the result of a single injury, like a fall or a lifting injury, or can develop gradually with repetitive overhead activity (long-term wear) like retrieving flies from overhead tree branches. Also, there's a bone called the acromion that's part of the shoulder anatomy which is directly over to rotator cuff. It evolved as a structure to help protect the cuff, but it can develop a spur on its underside that can wear a hole in the cuff over time...even with pretty normal use.

Personally, my rotator cuff isn't too bad, but I have friends who have had to undergo surgery just to keep casting a fly rod. The only surgeries I've had in order to keep fishing were a knee arthroscopy (torn cartilage...meniscus) and a carpal tunnel surgery. The knee was because I could no longer walk into the mountains. The carpal tunnel was because I couldn't cast or hold the rod for more than a minute without a lot of pain followed by complete loss of sensation in my thumb, index and middle finger on my dominant hand—even tried to learn to cast with my left hand.

The carpal tunnel is basically a narrow tunnel-like structure in the middle of the wrist.

The sides and bottom of the tunnel are formed by the carpal (wrist) bones. The top is covered by a strong band of tissue called the transverse carpal ligament. Through the tunnel travels the median nerve along with a bunch of flexor tendons. The median nerve controls feeling in the digits I just mentioned, and the muscles around the base of the thumb. Carpal tunnel syndrome occurs when the synovial tissue that surrounds the flexor tendons swells and puts pressure on the median nerve. The swelling narrows the already confined space in the tunnel and can crowd the nerve. Nerves hate to be crowded. Overuse, heredity and of course, age can cause the syndrome.

The good news is, carpal tunnel syndrome is pretty treatable, whether it's bracing, medications, injections or surgery.

One condition I've seen a lot with fly fishermen is De Quervain's Tendinitis. That's when the tendons around the base of the thumb are irritated or constricted. "Thickening" of the tendons can cause quite a bit of tenderness. It can become particularly painful when forming a fist, or when grasping or gripping things...like fly rods. De Quervain's can come on fast. I've taught and guided fly fishing for many years, and I've seen people inflicted on the second day of a three-day course. Most people hold the fly rod with their dominant hand with their thumb on top of the handle, pointing along the rod towards the tip. One can exert a little pressure on the handle near the end of the forward cast with the thumb which can help with the loop in the line as the fly hits the water...also the thumb can help with accuracy. But the thumb position in the grip is not etched in stone. Another other way to grip the rod is with a baseball grip, which eliminates pressure on the thumb almost altogether.

Unfortunately, if you get De Quervain's type symptoms on a fly fishing trip, there's no easy, quick fix. Anti-inflammatory meds might help, but avoiding the activity that causes the pain and swelling (like casting) would be the ticket. I've had two experiences with just that problem. Once, some buddies and I had planned a trip for peacock bass in Venezuela. One of the guys (whom we called "fish guts") got hit with the tendinitis quite badly. In our first aid kit we found an old wrist splint in the bottom of the kit that had some soft metal splints sewn into it. We ripped out one of the splints, bent it into a shape that would lay along the back of the thumb which held the digit in a neutral position, and padded it before taping it in place. It worked perfectly and Fish Guts fished the rest of the week relatively pain-free. It doesn't always work out that way for us.

Another time, I got a touch of the tendinitis near Heart Lake in the back country of Yellowstone. As soon as I realized what was going on I switched to a baseball grip, which was an unnatural feeling for me, but a lot more comfortable than full on De Quervain's Tendinitis.

A friend of mine once got a bad case of tennis elbow from casting big flies for muskies up on the St. John River. Lateral Epicondylitis can hurt like a son-of-a-gun and usually surprises people with the level of pain when they get it. It is an inflamation of the tendons that join the forearm muscles on the outside of the elbow. The forearm muscles and tendons become irritated from overuse...repeating the same motions again and again. Once again, it's all about repetitive activities and, you guessed it, *age*. Once you get a physician to diagnose it, more than 85% of tennis elbow sufferers have success with nonsurgical treatment. Rest often helps, but that would mean stopping fishing. There are anti-inflammatory meds that can help. Physical therapy also can in some cases and bracing is worth a try. I'd see an orthopedist if it gets bad. Sometimes, just fine-tuning your casting method a little can make a huge difference.

These are just some of the injuries fly fishers occasionally have to deal with, especially an older angler, whether they are hard-core or a novice. I can't speak to what injuries bait fishermen might get. Perhaps hooking each other with treble hooks, falling out of boats, or from fights with game wardens and park rangers. I don't know, maybe they never hurt themselves...only the fish.

Aging is a horrible disease, as much for a fly fisher as for anyone else. As we get older we have to deal with wading issues, sight problems, even access to the water can become a problem.

If you want to avoid some of those nasty, annoying inflammation-type injuries, you'll want to do two things...stay fit by doing low-impact exercises like biking, swimming or walking, and by practicing your casting to insure good mechanics.

We eventually, hopefully, get to a point in life when we need to consider fishing with a buddy, which has its own unique set of considerations. But it's definitely safer. We then will start thinking about hanging-up the old friend of a fly vest and going with a sling, chest pack or a belly pack. They're lighter, easier to manage and fit well with a PFD—possibly the most important gear change to consider as we get older and maybe a little unsteady on our feet, which we all know, jumps to another level when we're walking in rivers and streams. And no matter what, use a wading staff. Once total knee and hip replacements are thrown into the mix, we should probably start thinking about lakes, ponds and fishing from boats.

Loss of fishable water can occur as well. As we get older, obviously, time keeps on a-movin' and as time goes by, more people are getting into fly fishing. That's probably a good thing. In the last three years I've taught more people fly fishing than the seven years prior. Part of that is because when I was farming I didn't have as much time for classes. But with more people angling there's the chance that more bodies will be on the water at your favorite old spots. Last summer I was fishing my favorite stream in all of the Eastern United States, down in the blueberry barrens in Washington County, a place I've fished for forty years. I saw other fishermen there for the first time in all those years. Two of them. They were throwing worms. Oh, it didn't bother me much, it's every bit their right, but later that evening I couldn't help but feel that I'd lost a little bit of my own history. Of course I hadn't, but it felt real enough.

Why do people who fly fish seem so passionate about it? Why do so many people who fly fish want to write about it, read about it, and write poems about it? Because I believe that once you try it—if it takes root—it is so beautiful, so rewarding in a natural way that more than any other sport, it becomes more like a gift than a sport, or a hobby, or a pastime. Those who fly fish see in fishing something more. Something lovely. If angling with fly tackle—or the love of it—is indeed a gift, then maybe *that* should be the point as we get older. Maybe we should gift it to someone else. So what if they end up on our old, favorite waters. They're not really our waters anyway, are they?

And one other thing...the older you get, the more important it is to remember to pee just before you put on your waders.

El Camino Real

Not-so-gentle fish and Conquistadores

Pleasant River Lake, Maine 2010

I've been writing off and on for many years and I swore I would never start an essay with, *"There I was, (blah blah blah)"* or include a photograph of myself kneeling in a river, holding my fly rod and a big trout, with a stupid grin on my face. So far so good.

Anyway…there I was, standing on the banks of a small stream in the steaming, dark Darien jungle, dripping with sweat and mud, wondering what in hell smelled so bad. It was horrific. It was worse than a camel fart (they are hard to describe) and I could feel the stink deep in my sinuses. It took a little while to realize it was coming from my feet.

I had purchased a brand-new pair of Merrill hiking shoes three days before leaving for Panama. They are the only brand of hikers I've tried in thirty years that require no breaking in whatsoever. You can take them off the shelf, lace 'em up and live in them without running the risk of ever getting a blister.

Now, six days later, they were the foulest smelling things on the planet. They were the only shoes I had with me, so for the next six days at least I would have to suck it up and live with the stench. I had hired a local Miskito Indian named Florinda from the port town of Portobelo to help carry some of the gear like the metal detector and the tent.

To this day I don't know what made him cry...the smell from my feet, or the fact that I had forgotten to bring any coffee, but the jovial, forty-year-old man definitely struggled a bit. Oh, he didn't outright cry, but for a couple of days his lips curled at the corners and with furrowed brow he'd say, "...no café?" all the while glancing at my feet and then back at my face. It was pretty clear he was thinking, "And now I've gone off into the jungle with this retarded gringo."

It was 1986 and I was lucky enough to snag a photography job for the Department of Tourism of Panama. For about three weeks I had the run of the country...helicopters, boats, jeeps...whatever I needed to make the images I would need for the layout of a new tourism brochure. Sweet deal, indeed. But, as usual, my brain got in the way, and when the good Mr. Pinto from the Department of Tourism said I could, after the shoot was finished, stay in country with a per diem, I started to scheme. What if, I thought, I could shoot some more of my favorite stuff and maybe go on a little adventure?

Living in Peru for a while had taught me about the devastation laid upon that country by the conquistadors in the 1500's. I knew that much of the plunder for decades had been shipped north to Old Panama City and then hauled on the backs of burros along a "paved" road across the Isthmus of Panama to the east coast. Once there, the treasure was either smelted down or packed up and shipped off to finance the Spanish Empire. Parts of the road are lost to history, and to the jungle. I figured I had a great opportunity to find a portion of it. It would be very cool if I could, and in those days cool was good enough reason to do just about anything.

I left a good portion of my gear which I wouldn't need on this little "mini-expedition" at the hotel in Panama City and took to bus to Portobelo. It was a good bus, not the rickety old death traps so common in some Latin American countries. We wound slowly out of the sprawling city, through some pretty farmland with decrepit cinder-block houses and eventually dropped into some "light" jungle habitat. I was riding through the jungle, no doubt, but this was *not* the Darien I was heading for, said by some to be the densest jungle vegetation in the world. (I'm not sure about that...it's definitely denser than the Manus in Peru, but I would have to argue for the border between Brazil and Venezuela. I've never been in the jungles of Africa that I saw in all the Tarzan shows as a kid.)

The bus eventually gained elevation as we headed east back into more farm country, each pasture surrounded by vast tracts of forestation which looked like jungle to me. Once we hit the coast, we turned south and dropped into the town of Portobelo. A port city of around 3,000 folks from throughout the Caribe, it was built on and around the Spanish fortifications that overlook the harbor. Snug little homes are built along the waterfront and quite often a pitted old cannon sticks out from between back porches, still trained on the horizon waiting for that old pirate Captain Morgan.

I love Portobelo. Most of its citizens are black, but as a white guy from Maine (living in Boston) I never felt the least bit out of water. More than anywhere I've ever been, I felt the calming and comfortable sense of not being judged. Many of the locals are Congos...descendants of the Cimarrones—runaway slaves who fought rather bravely during the Spanish colonial days. They escaped their captives, fled into the jungle and built fortified villages. They were so good at fighting the Spaniards (who were known to be a bit cruel, at times) that the former enslavers eventually met with the Cimarrones and said, "ah...O.K., you're free." Somewhere along the way, the people of Portobelo evolved into a kind, peaceable, accepting, happy group of people. Or perhaps they always have been.

I went into a little store for a few groceries my first day there when some music erupted outside. I remember sticking my head out of the doorway to watch some people dancing by in fancy, colorful, and flamboyant costumes. A boy about twelve years old lunged at me as if trying to scare me and yelled something like "Hey!"...but he was smiling. He shoved a small wooden box in my face and flipped open the cover which revealed a model of an amputated human penis, and a little bloody guillotine. I couldn't help but take it as a bad sign. As it turned out, my trip coincided with the Festival of the Devil. It's a celebration of their self-deliverance from slavery, the triumph of good over evil, their African heritage, and a few other things that were a little blurry for me. It was great...great food, great costumes and great fun. Some years ago it became a bigger, more popular festival called Diablos and Congos and is quite the tourist attraction. In 1980 the Spanish fortification at Portobelo was made a UNESCO World Heritage site.

Within three hours I found a house to rent for a week, complete with a cute young housekeeper with a gold tooth which she must have been pretty proud of, because I never saw her when she wasn't smiling. It was one of the houses with its own cannon in the back yard and there was a great screened-in porch about forty feet from the water and a big hammock hanging from the ceiling. There were also a couple of divers from Iowa staying in the house and a tiny black and white stray cat that would not leave me alone. If I could have gotten her by customs I would have brought her home with me—the cat...not the housekeeper.

Once settled, I walked around town and began the task of finding someone who is good in the jungle. There was way too much gear to carry for one person to make any real headway in the humid, hot jungle. I knew that much. I asked the SCUBA boys if they had met any likely people, but they had no idea. They knew where both the pubs were though, and what time they opened. I found a municipal building but it was closed. I went to the bus station but they were no help at all. I went to the only pub I could find, but the tender didn't know of anyone so I had a beer. On the way back to the house I ran into smiling Maria the housekeeper trotting down the hill. I asked her and she told me about this friend of a friend named Florinda who would have the time to go (whatever that meant) and that she would have him meet me in the morning at the Customs House. She told me all that without ever losing the smile and I never lost sight of the gold tooth.

About nine the next morning I lumbered down the hill to the Customs House, and there was my guy, squatting against the outside of the ancient stone wall. I suspected right away there might be a language problem because his bright yellow T-shirt said Daddy's Little Girl in big black letters. My poor Spanish and his poor English were good enough to get by, and we agreed on a price for a weeks' worth of carrying gear. He would meet me at the rented house in three days. That would give me a day for some world class snorkeling and to organize the gear. I was pretty jazzed for the trip, but I could tell by his expressions and his body language he thought I had no idea what I was doing, but that we would probably live through the ordeal anyway.

Here's the best part: the map I had was a copy of a chart dated 1750 when the road ended in Nombre de Dios, about twenty miles from Portobelo. Armed with that old map and a handful of notes from explorers and those of a friend who had found what he was sure were flagstones in a "non-flagstone environment," we started out early in the morning. Some of the gear was awkward to carry while wearing a big backpack. Since I was used to living out of a pack, and carrying about eighty pounds, I carried about twice the weight that Florinda did. According to my journal, I carried the tent, camera gear, the machete, my sleeping bag, a sleeping pad, a mosquito net, the maps and notes, water filter with bottles, my clothes, binoculars, some plastic collecting jars, a box of flies, my 4-weight G. Loomis fly rod, and enough food for eight days. Florinda carried a sleeping pad, his own machete, a mosquito net, his own water jug, a mountaineering gas stove that weighs less than a pound, a half-liter fuel bottle, his clothes (which he brought with him in a plastic grocery bag), my submersible White metal detector, and the mess kit. It all fit into a backpack I had borrowed from a friend I knew in Panama City. It was a woman's pack and fit him perfectly.

I failed to mention to Florinda how unlikely it was that the trip would be successful, but it must have been apparent…at no point did he exhibit any faith that we would find anything significant.

When the Spanish Empire was systematically conquering, colonizing and plundering the New World, they needed a way to get the gold and untold treasure across the Isthmus of Panama. They tried navigating rivers, but they were too shallow and unpredictable, and to this day it's not possible. The only navigable waterway was the Chagre River, which could be ascended in winter, but only to within about twenty miles from Panama City. The history of the area is amazing, filled with sea battles, overland campaigns, bushwhacking, big pirate names, conquistadores, and lost treasures. The original Royal Road, the "Camino Real," did connect Panama (Panama City) to the eastern port of Nombre de Dios, but was later moved to Portobelo about the time Francisco Pizzaro was raping Peru. Portobelo had a much more navigable and defendable harbor. For nearly 300 years, El Camino Real was the most important highway in the Spanish Main. The road was built by slaves, of course, paved with flat stones harvested from stream beds. It was wide enough for two carts to pass and wound through some of the densest jungle on the planet. It must have been a logistical nightmare, but it was probably more appealing than sailing plunder-laden ships around the Horn. Pirates sometimes anchored out in the harbor at Portobelo. In one old Spaniard's journal, the soldier mentions that his officers couldn't believe how ostentatious the pirates were. Sir Francis Drake arrived in 1573, did his pillaging thing for a while until he died in '96 from dysentery and was buried in a lead coffin, dumped into the harbor. After Drake, Boss Pirate of the Caribbean was assumed by Captain Henry Morgan, a belligerent drunk who took Portobelo in 1668. He plundered all he could find, then raped and tortured the inhabitants. He stayed for two weeks and before he left he burned the town and spiked the cannon in the fort. In 1670, Morgan led his murderous gang across the isthmus to Panama Viejo, bushwhacking mule trains along the way. The Spanish were royally pissed off, and eventually abandoned El Camino Real, surrendering it to the jungle. It was just too hard to defend in the Darien.

One of the many legends swirling around the country when I was on the photo assignment was of the Viper Pits. Viper Pits is an exciting name, but they're really nothing more than steep areas of the narrow road that would become slippery when wet. Now and then a burrow or mule, heavy with treasure, would slip, fall and plummet into the river below. The Indian slaves, believing there were vipers in the waters below, would refuse to go after the gold. The Spaniards would write off the loss and continue on their way. If one could find the road, and some steep, precarious sections, it's feasible one could find some treasure, right? Sure. At least, I would fish.

I won't go into detail here about the exact whereabouts of the beginning of the old road. It would be hard to explain in writing, but I will say access is 1,000 paces from the King's Customs House. The beginning of the trek is through fertile, coastal farmland. The beautiful blue Caribbean framed bright green pastures bordered by tall, slightly bent palm trees.

It was an inauspicious start. As we made a beeline towards the jungle, we had to cut through one of the farm pastures. We scrambled over a low, barbed wire fence and put the Caribe to our backs, heading south-southwest. Halfway across the field, Florinda noticed a big black bull with those Texas longhorn-type horns. He looked...interested. I have no idea if the color red actually does anything to incite a bull, or if it's some kind of myth, but the metal detector I had strapped to Florinda's back was packed in its scarlet canvas bag. I tapped my guy's shoulder, pointed to the bull, then at the red bag. Florinda's eyes widened and he bolted for the fence. I looked back and sure enough, that bull was jogging toward us. I bolted too. I couldn't help noticing that Flo went *through* the fence, not over it. The bull never really attacked us, and Florinda was relatively unscathed, but it was exciting for a few moments.

I love jungles, which is weird because it seems everything in them can (and will) bite, sting, stick or suck you. There are poisonous insects, frogs and plants. There are deadly eyelash vipers, fer-de-lances and, my personal favorites, leeches. And there is unspeakable beauty that can only be understood by experiencing the real thing.

As we progressed deeper into the darkness, I reconsidered the Darien being the densest jungle on the planet, and I think that's probably correct. The vegetation is "thicker" than in the Manus of Peru and that of the Brazilian/Venezuelan frontier (but no easier to walk through than the puckerbrush of northern Maine). The main difference noted in my journal was the terrain. If we weren't in a swamp (which we avoided, same as the Spaniards and the English pirates), then we were negotiating precipitous crags, camouflaged with vines and other vegetation.

Within ten minutes of wacking our way into the jungle proper, I was soaked with sweat, and would stay that way for a week. At night I would change into semi-dry sleeping clothes and hang the wet ones up to dry, then back into damp clothes each morning. In those days I always used quick-drying tropical clothing from the Patagonia Company, which helped a lot. I was partial to Patagonia clothes because years earlier in Jackson Hole, Wyoming, I had met Yvonne Chouinard briefly after a very uncomfortable bivouac on the South Teton when he said, softly, "...things are a lot more fun when you're warm and dry." I'm sure he wouldn't remember that, but I never forgot it.

There were streams everywhere it seemed. Most were tributaries to the Portobelo River and we camped along one of them every night. I hadn't planned on fishing until we got further inland. I didn't fish, but it was tough because many times as we walked up onto a stream we would see fish scoot away from us in the pools. They were small fish, and I figured they would be, which is why I brought the 4-weight.

Florinda must have had some experience guiding eco-tourists, for he kept scurrying around bringing me insects and leaves and pointing out birds and spiders. I hadn't expected or asked him to do that, but I loved it. I collected some of the insects, but mostly took photos and notes for later identification. He knew I was specifically looking for El Camino Real, though. When he would see me looking around during breaks, poking under bushes for any paving stones, he would raise both eyebrows, look astonished and say *"Oro!"* as if he had just discovered a treasure chest.

Every day filled up our senses. On the third day it rained for a couple hours midday, and we kept on walking because we couldn't have gotten any wetter anyway. That afternoon, just like I've seen in old Hollywood movies, I was taking my turn in the lead, wacking with the machete, taking a step and wacking some more. I wacked, stepped and was suddenly jerked backward as Florinda yanked hard on my backpack...my right foot purposefully sticking out over a 100-foot cliff. Wounds can turn septic in an hour in the Darien, and if I'd taken the fall it would have been curtains. I didn't think people actually accidentally walked off cliffs like that. Oh, and incidentally...I did it again the following day, and Florinda grabbed me again. I felt like such a putz.

On our fourth day—our turn-around day— Florinda pointed to a bird. He heard it first and stalked it for a bit. I got two photographs and later identified it as a Golden-Headed Quetzal. It wasn't supposed to be at such a low elevation I'm told...but there he was. He was beautiful, with his bright red chest and abdomen, his green throat and shoulders, dark wings, and mustard-yellow head. (That spicy-brown mustard, not the bright yellow kind.) I remember late that night I had to get up for a leak and as I arose from the tent door, I stood in wonder, perplexed by the thousands of fireflies that lit up the dark night. There may have been millions. I wanted to wake Florinda, but thought he may have seen them hundreds of times, so I just sat on a log by the stream and stared at them for a half hour. I get perplexed kinda easily. I wondered if 500 years ago some soldier sat there and saw the same thing, and if he did, was he just as awed as I was?

In the mornings we would awake to the guttural cries of the brilliant blue and green macaws. Every morning, a multitude of scarlet and blue butterflies fluttered about and sunned themselves like an explosion of color against the dark green foliage.

On the afternoon of the fifth day, while making camp on an unnamed stream, I happened to see a half dozen fish dart upstream into a pool. I could tell they would be stuck in the pool because of a six-foot waterfall. It didn't take long to get the 4-weight rigged. I happened to know what color the leeches were along the stream, because I'm pretty sure they were the same kind I had been plucking off my arms and neck for the past four days. So a size 10 Black Woolly Bugger it was.

The casting was easy enough; I just stepped out onto some rocks in the middle of the stream below the pool. If the fish wanted to leave, they would have to swim right by me in about a foot of water. The head of the pool was maybe eighty feet upstream, and to the right was a little eddy and what looked like deeper water, about four to six feet deep.

I made the cast straight upstream into the seam between the edge of the eddy and the main current, and I can tell you, I wasn't ready for the "take." It was...scary. The fly hit the water, sank a little, I stripped in twice and the water kind of exploded. At first I thought it was some huge leviathan, hidden in the jungle stream, but it only took a moment to realize it was in fact, about five small fish fighting over the fly. One was hooked, and it fought like hell. It jumped, thrashed and bolted like any great gamefish. I had caught peacock bass in Gatun Lake to the north, and in Venezuela, but I hadn't expected catching one in that stream. When I finally landed it, rather unceremoniously by dragging it onto the little beach, I was surprised to see that it wasn't a peacock at all. About fourteen inches long, it was shaped a little like a peacock bass, with a really long dorsal fin with seventeen to eighteen spines, it was golden-green with purplish and black markings and a mouth a bit like a tarpon's when its lips were extended. It had bright red eyes. Florinda wanted to eat it, but I released it anyway. He said he never saw one before, and, as crazy as it sounds, I thought if there is a fish poisonous to eat, it would probably be in that place.

I caught six or seven more before they either moved on or wised up. It wasn't until I got stateside and found the time to do a little research, that I found out they were actually Jaguar Guapote, a popular aquarium fish. Reading about them, I remember the recurring theme of "aggressive," and "fighting and territorial." Sounded about right. Like the Quetzal, they weren't supposed to be in that part of the jungle. Someone was confused, either the animals or the people writing about them.

We stuck to my primitive plan to take a compass bearing NNW straight through about a mile of jungle to connect with another small stream, and then follow it downstream back to the east coast and hitchhike south to Portobelo. It looked reasonable on a map, but ended up being one of those things I underestimated in the planning. The idea was that we might possibly bisect the Camino Real or find some sign of it along the new stream, if we hadn't already and didn't even know it. The map I had wasn't the best of topo maps and the contours weren't real accurate. A "dip" on the map was a chasm in reality, and a gentle rise in elevation was a cliff. We did a lot of diverting, scooting, and scrambling, and a *lot* of hacking with machetes. That mile took us hours and when we did find the stream, it was about half the size shown on the map. At most, it was about twelve feet across, so I was disappointed because of the lack of fishable water. I did try a few deeper pools as we got closer to the coast, but couldn't get a single rise. I tried the woolly buggers, some stimulaters, and some big stonefly nymphs. Nothing. The truth is, I can tell by my journal that after eight days in the jungle, I may have been too beat up and tired to fish.

We never did find the Camino Real. For me the road remained a lost part of the historic Spanish Main. It was a beautiful adventure which took three days to recover from in Portobelo.

In eight days, I lost twenty-one pounds and a brand new pair of Merrill hiking shoes. When I got back home in Boston, I had my feet checked out at Mass General Hospital to make sure whatever fungus invaded my shoes wasn't lingering on the skin of my feet, regardless of how many times a day I scrubbed them with soap and water. The resident Doc that examined me, treated them prophylactically with some fungicide pills and they were fine. There was one leech wound on the back of my shoulder that had gotten infected and needed to be cleaned out. It required dressing changes, twice a day for a couple of weeks, which basically sucked. I couldn't reach it and I found out who my friends were.

Even though we found no Spanish road and Florinda found no treasure chest, we did find unbelievable beauty, some pristine jungle with amazing sights, and some pretty interesting camaraderie. During my eight days in the Darien I got to catch fish for a total of about ten hours, and caught some of the hardest-fighting aquarium fish ever, pound for pound. Pretty cool. Would I go back and do it all again? You bet...but I'd take some back-up shoes. Oh, and I'd do *something* about those Goddamned leeches.

www.ingramcontent.com/pod-product-compliance
Lightning Source LLC
Chambersburg PA
CBHW031835090426
42741CB00005B/248